CLASSIC SCIENCE FICTION

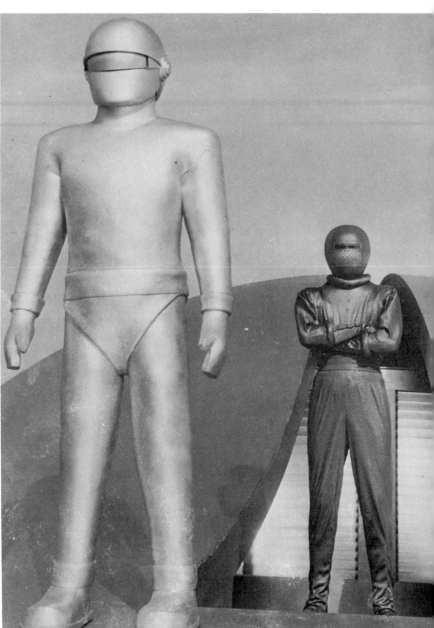

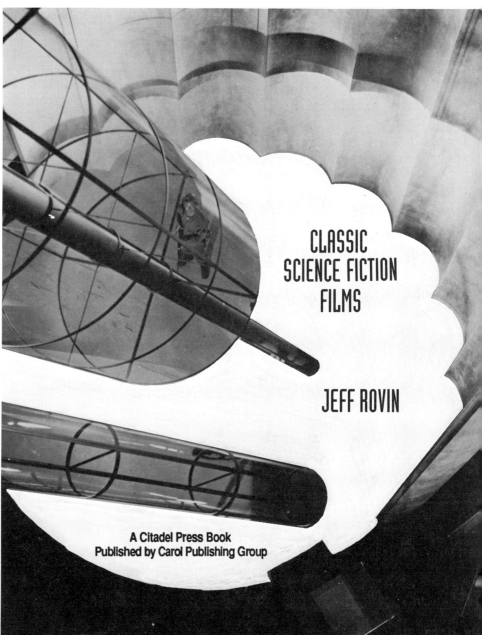

CLASSIC SCIENCE FICTION FILMS

JEFF ROVIN

A Citadel Press Book
Published by Carol Publishing Group

Dedicated to Ray Harryhausen

Carol Publishing Group Edition - 1993

A Citadel Press Book
Published by Carol Publishing Group
Citadel Press is a registered trademark of
Carol Communications, Inc.

Editorial Offices:
600 Madison Avenue
New York, NY 10022

Sales & Distribution Offices:
120 Enterprise Avenue
Secaucus, NJ 07094

In Canada: Canadian Manda Group
P.O. Box 920, Station U
Toronto, Ontario, M8Z 5P9, Canada

Queries regarding rights and permissions should be addressed to:
Carol Publishing Group
600 Madison Avenue, New York, NY 10022

Designed by Peretz Kaminsky

Manufactured in the United States of America
ISBN 0-8065-1463-9

Carol Publishing Group books are available at special discounts for bulk purchases,
for sales promotions, fund raising, or educational purposes. Special editions can also
be created to specifications. For details contact: Special Sales Department, Carol
Publishing Group, 120 Enterprise Ave., Secaucus, NJ 07094

Library of Congress catalog card number: 74-29544

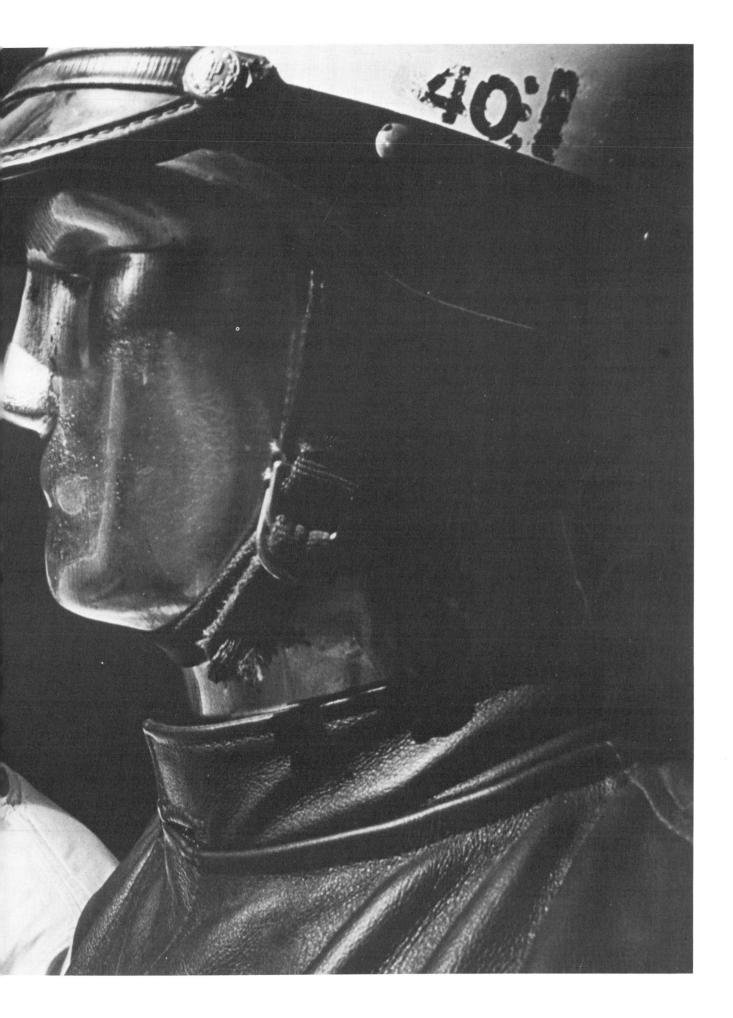

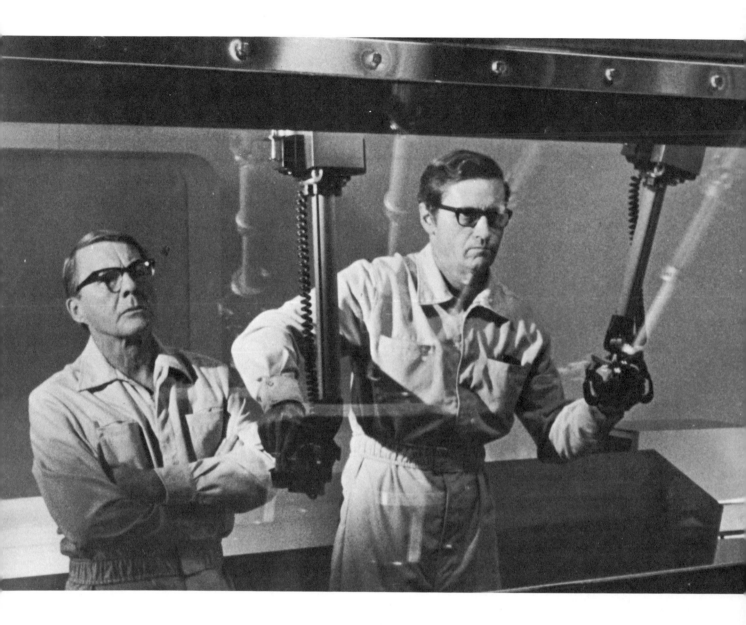

Acknowledgments

Photographs supplied by Allan Asherman, from the Asherman Archives.
All rights reserved.

Sincere thanks and appreciation to the following studios for their generous cooperation:

Allied Artists, American International Productions, Animated Industries, Avco Embassy Productions, The BBC, Columbia Pictures Corporation, 20th Century-Fox, Metro-Goldwyn-Mayer, Hammer Films, Toho Productions, RKO, Paramount Pictures, United Artists, National Periodical Publications, Universal Pictures, Warner Bros., Walt Disney Productions, ABC, CBS, and NBC.

Special thanks are in order to Leslie Stevens, who, among other things, lent me her desk.

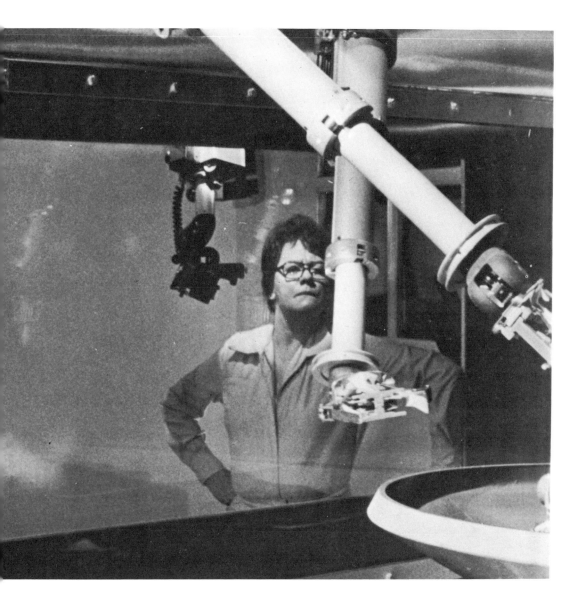

Contents

Introduction

A look at *the world-that-was from* Things to Come.

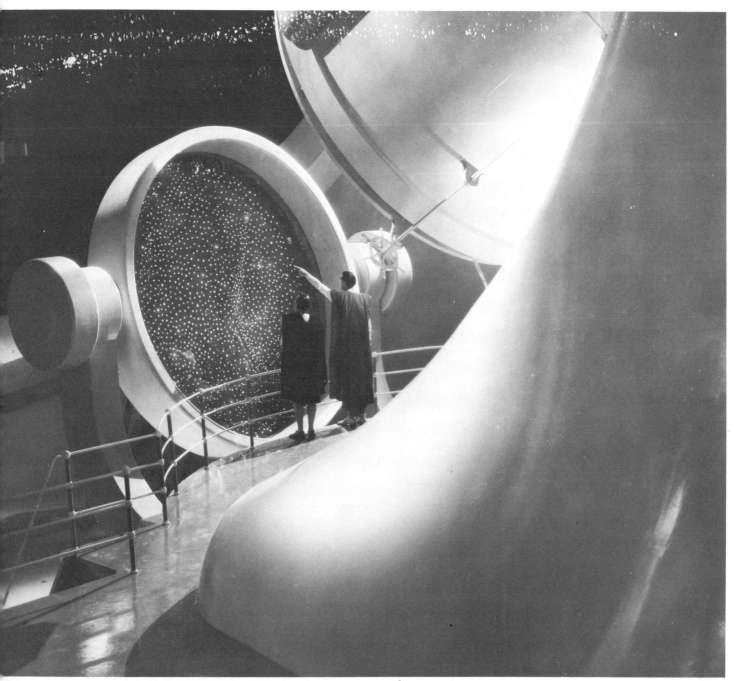

*The Frankenstein Monster as he
appeared in the original 1910
Edison Company production,
Frankenstein.*

Science fiction is, at best, a very subjective label. It is easy enough to call a film like *Fantastic Voyage* or *Marooned* science fiction, but what of *Frankenstein?* Certainly it is based in scientific speculation; yet most people would call it a horror film. We have included it in this book, along with such films as *The Time Machine* and *Twenty Thousand Leagues under the Sea,* even though many aficionados would consider these not science fiction, but fantasy. That the several genres overlap there is obviously no doubt. It is therefore best that people build their own definitions. However, these personal boundaries are so diverse that it would be impossible to please everyone. Thus, for our purposes, science fiction will be broadly defined as any science-based event that has not occurred but conceivably could, given the technology of the period in which a film is set.

In our text we malign many films, but we love *all* science-fiction films, from the markedly absurd (like *King Kong vs. Godzilla*), to the technically inept (like *King Dinosaur*), to the awful (like *Frankenstein Meets the Space Monster*), to the profound (like *2001: A Space Odyssey*), to the spectacular (like *Forbidden Planet*). There is something about the genre —perhaps its loving tolerance for the patently fantastic—that is refreshing in a world where exactitude and precision are pursued with feverish deliberation and imagination and flights of fancy are frowned upon by the masses as impractical. It is for this reason, too, that we have not attempted any weighty dissertations on science fiction as a social mirror or psychological showcase. There are books enough of that sort already. These volumes dissect science fiction and make a shambles of its beauty. Take any living entity and dissect it, analyze it, tear it to pieces, and categorize the parts—and you no longer have a useful whole; what remain are only pieces that can be interpreted, and reassembled, often in many different ways.

So although we may trace the origins or *raison d'être* for a particular film, we entertain no discussions about how Morbius' Id in *Forbidden Planet* foreshadowed Mothra's victory over Godzilla in *Godzilla vs. the Thing* or how *The Beast from Twenty Thousand Fathoms* is really Touchbottom from *A Midsummer Night's Dream*. Of course, anyone can read a message into a film: for example, critics have recently chosen to see King Kong as the black man rebelling against white oppression. There is a case for this if one is inclined to look at things that way, but this book is an entertainment, rather than a lofty critical document. It is informal, hardly pedantic, and created solely for the enjoyment of the lay reader and interested fan.

Ray Harryhausen, to whom this work is dedicated, is one of the most prominent members of the science-fiction community. Mr. Harryhausen is the medium's greatest special-effects man; his work in such films as *Twenty Million Miles to Earth* and *Seventh Voyage of Sinbad* remain the finest examples of screen wizardry in history. And thanks are in order to Allan Asherman, without whose contribution this book could never have been created. Al supplied all the photographs, offered information on many of the films, and wrote the remarkably perceptive first draft of the discussion of *Things to Come*.

We have chosen to emphasize certain films in this volume's pictorial section. You will notice, for instance, a plethora of stills from *Forbidden Planet, When Worlds Collide, Planet of the Apes,* and *2001: A Space Odyssey.* All photographs were chosen for their historical and entertainment value, as well as the interest they would likely generate. Thus, if you are a fan of *Catwoman of the Moon* or *Reptilicus,* you have been slighted. Forgive us.

The wreckage of an ancient vessel far beneath the Mysterious Island.

An undersea diver meets with the amphibious denizens of the 1929 Mysterious Island.

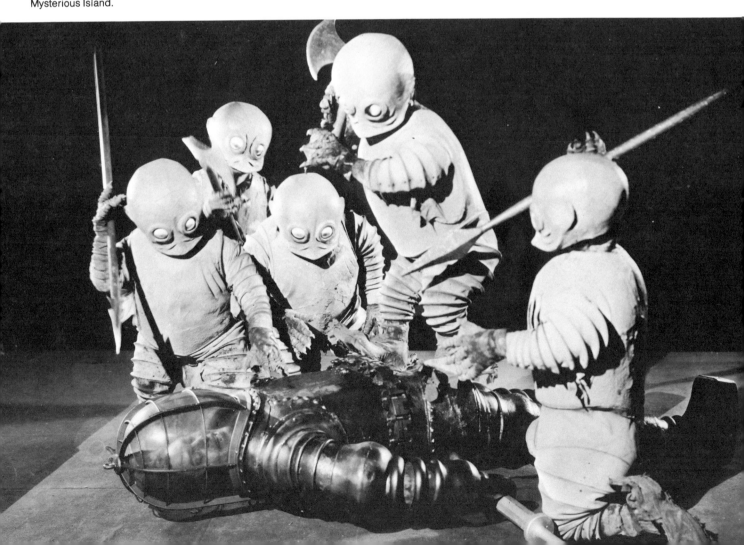

The Silents

"Worth the loss of a hand," cries Rotwang, whose robot will soon mesmerize all the subterranean inhabitants of Metropolis.

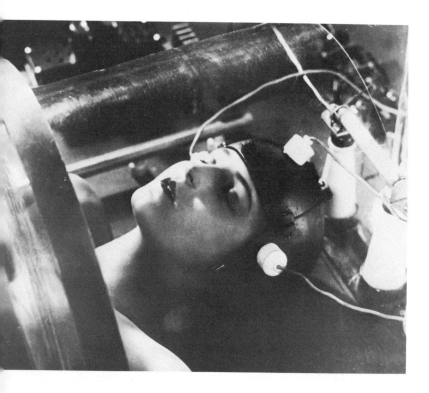

Rotwang's robot is transformed into a traitorous duplicate of Maria. From Metropolis.

After listening to a sermon given by the merciful Maria, Freder pledges her his assistance. From Metropolis.

One of the great science-fiction films, and certainly the most striking of all silent films, is the 1925 Fritz Lang epic *Metropolis*. *Metropolis* tells of Freder, son of John Fredersen, Master of Metropolis, a sprawling city of the future. We follow the young man's journey from the glittering towers of upper Metropolis to the murky, sunless catacombs of subterranean Metropolis. The trip is inspired by Maria, a subterranean who, with a group of sickly children from underground, visits Freder in his luxurious decadence and proclaims, "These are your brothers!"

Freder is unnerved by the inference that conditions under which the youngsters live are bestial compared with the surface dwellers' comfortable state. Curious and not unmoved, the young man visits the underworld and watches in horror as the inhabitants of the hellish catacombs operate the machinery that makes Metropolis tick. Utter degradation reigns, but there is Maria, preaching a gospel of a coming deliverer to give the people hope.

Not surprisingly, Fredersen fears the charismatic Maria, envisioning a time when she will thoroughly undermine his rule. Fredersen hires the genius Rotwang to create a robot Maria, indistinguishable from the original, and uses her to lead the subterraneans in revolt. Through revolution, Fredersen hopes, the rebellious element will destroy the machines and, thus, themselves.

Indeed, the destruction of monster machine Moloch causes the reservoirs to burst, flooding the entire underground. Maria and Freder manage to rescue the workers' children, the workers rescue themselves, and a just peace is established, with Freder's influence, between Fredersen and the subterraneans.

"The heart (Freder) must mediate between the brain (Fredersen) and the hands (the workers)," explains a closing title.

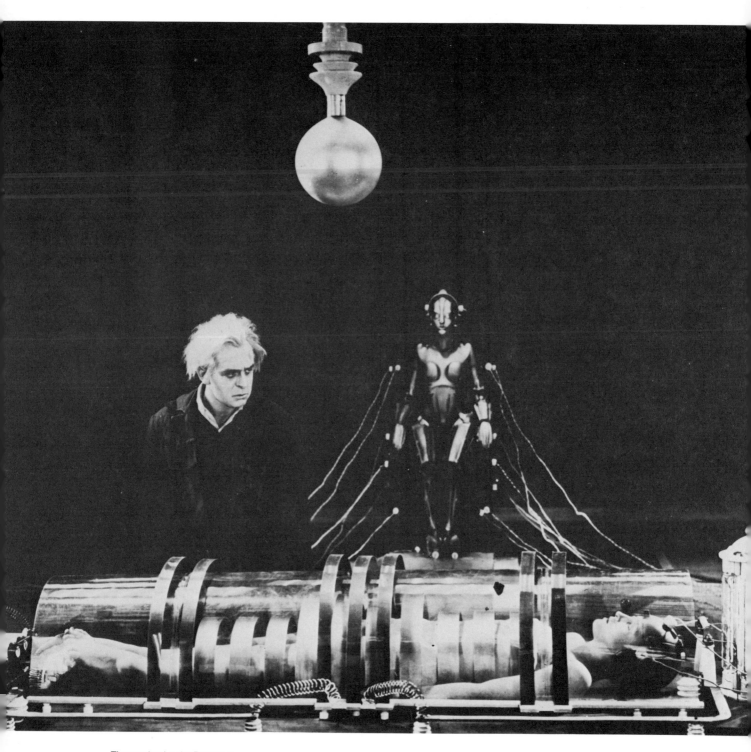

The mad scientist Rotwang prepares to bring his robotrix to life. From Metropolis.

Technically the film remains one of cinema's most striking achievements. The acting is incredible, and the flood scenes are beyond description. The art direction, special effects, and photography are flawless. Critics quibble about the purity of author Thea von Harbou's theme, perhaps equating it with a black-and-white Disneyesque philosophy, but it is an honest theme, worthy of our attention. The final idyllic harmony of Metropolis is beyond human capacities, but that is unimportant; it is an example of human excellence that is surely worth emulating.

Mr. Lang returned to science fiction with *Girl in the Moon* (1929), a tantalizing film about the first moon landing that was accurate as contemporary technology would allow. The film has since become dated, and what appear, today, blatant fallacies—such as author von Harbou's giving the moon a substantial atmosphere—can be overlooked because of the film's skill and presence of character, created by Lang.
In addition to the finesse of the Lang films, credit for bravura and for one of the most prolific imaginations in film history must go to the great French filmmaker Georges Méliès. Méliès, a former magician, went into film with the idea of transposing his magical arts to the screen. The results were often crude; it would be unjust, however, to discredit Méliès' work because of the medium's technical limitations. Indeed, Méliès deserves credit for *using* the visual potential of film to a greater degree, and with more rampant enthusiasm, than anyone before or after him, Disney and Kubrick notwithstanding.

In *Conquest of the Pole* (1912) and, especially, *A Trip to the Moon* (1902), Méliès, with little thought for camera movement and in very theatrical fashion, uses his special effects, sets, costumes, and art direction to a wildly imaginative degree. The films are weak in terms of polish but make up for this lack with their vivacity and vigor. No science-fiction-film maker since has quite equaled Méliès' charming tongue-in-cheek approach to the genre, and the line of bathing beauties that ignites the fuse sending Méliès and company on *A Trip to the Moon* back in 1902 remains classic.

While science fictionless fantasies such as *Dream of a Rarebit Fiend* (1906)[1] abound, *Aelita* (1924) and *Mysterious Island* (1929) can accurately bear the label science fiction.

Aelita is a lavishly accoutered film wherein Aelita, the queen of Mars, falls in love with Los, the first Russian cosmonaut, while Los's assistant, Gusev, is inciting the Martians to revolt against the dictatorship that makes them veritable slaves. This film, like most Soviet fantasy and science fiction, is mature and was created with sincerity and a respect for the medium and the genre.

Mysterious Island, featuring Lionel Barrymore under the sea, is notable for its impressive set design and use of a crude form of Technicolor.

These silent science-fiction epics established a fantastic-film identity that helped pave the way for the thirties and for a film acknowledged by most fans and critics as the finest science-fiction film ever made—*Things to Come.*

*A look at things to come: A
beautiful post-war city.*

*The bombed-out shell of a city in
Things to Come*

The two lovers of Things to Come.

Margaretta Scott in Things to Come.

Science fiction is a much-ridiculed medium, labeled by many people as tripe. Despite such films as *Metropolis, Forbidden Planet,* and *Planet of the Apes,* science fiction is second-class in the minds of many. This attitude can be explained only as unenlightenment on the part of the public. The logic that since science fiction deals with the future, it has no foothold on reality and is therefore useless and trivial, reflects a lack of constructive vision that has caught the public unaware in times of war, famine, and epidemic. This is not unusual. In 1936, had the public truly heeded the warning of H. G. Wells' frighteningly prophetic *Things to Come,* who knows how different the world might today have been?

Children play, oblivious to the impending catastrophe of warfare. From Things to Come.

Moral speculation aside, *Things to Come* is a striking and exciting motion picture, and the technical difficulties encountered in its production are typical of those faced and conquered by science fiction film makers since Georges Méliès. A detailed look behind the scenes will provide some idea of what it takes to make a great science fiction film.

In the film, world war erupts in the then-present, and continues for decade upon decade, its brutality shown in the microcosmic city of "Everytown." Eventually the larger countries disintegrate, leaving small warring tribes to perpetuate the strife.

A society of super scientific minds, headed by John Cabal (Raymond Massey), seeks to end the world war. And, by the year 2036, peace has been restored. However, internal unrest in Everytown threatens to evaporate this peace, and tempers flare when the ruler, Oswald Cabal (Raymond Massey), son of John, proposes to send his daughter and the son of his friend Passworthy into space.

Sculptor Theotocopulous (Cedric Hardwicke) seeks a return to the simple life and therefore heads a mob against Cabal and his "space gun." But the assault comes too late, and the pair is launched into space. As Cabal and Passworthy watch, they philosophize:

A view of the giant space gun and its manned projectile. From Things to Come.

View of the intricate earth-digging machinery used to rebuild the war-devastated world of Things to Come.

PASSWORTHY: I feel that what we've done is monstrous!

CABAL: What we've done is magnificent.

PASSWORTHY: If they don't come back—my son and your daughter—what of that, Cabal?

CABAL: Then, presently, others will go.

PASSWORTHY: Oh, God, is there ever to be any age of happiness? Is there never to be any rest?

CABAL: Rest enough for the individual man—too much, and too soon—and we call it death. But for Man [kind], no rest and no ending. He must go on, conquest beyond conquest. First this little planet with its winds and ways, and then all the laws of mind and matter that restrain him. Then the planets about him, and at last out across immensity to the stars. And when he has conquered all the deeps of space and all the mysteries of time, still he will be beginning.

PASSWORTHY: But . . . we're such little creatures. Poor humanity's so fragile, so weak. Little . . . little animals.

CABAL: Little animals. If we're no more than animals, we must snatch each little scrap of happiness and live and suffer and pass, mattering no more than all the other animals do or have done. Is it this—or that (*pointing to the spaceship now visible on the space mirror*): all the universe or nothingness. Which shall it be, Passworthy? Which shall it be?

Things to Come is atypical from every conceivable standpoint, but especially because it is the product of a union between two geniuses of different media. As with 1968's *2001: A Space Odyssey*, in which the guiding forces were producer-director Stanley Kubrick and author Arthur C. Clarke, *Things to Come* owes its being to producer Alexander Korda and author H. G. Wells.

Wells had begun his literary career as a journalist, reporting on news that was shaping the world. Gradually, he branched into subsidiary fields. He became an eminent historian as

Raymond Massey as the super-scientific bringer-of-peace in Things to Come.

Ad-art for Things to Come.

*Pre and post launch preparations
for the manned spacecraft
launched in* Things to Come.

well as a fiction writer, and his two-volume *Outline of History* is definitive. In *Things to Come*, the English socialist tackled a far more difficult task in penning a history yet to come. Wells drew upon historical antecedents, sprinkled these with current events and likely trends, and wrote what appeared most likely to be the course of history at that time. A credit to Wells' boundless gifts, it was no problem for the author to transcribe a hundred years of theory from his mind's eye to paper and indeed, by the time the novel eventually became a screenplay, Wells' portrait of the future was incredibly accurate.

Wells wrote the screenplay, but the first draft was so vast in scope and so ponderous in length that Korda simultaneously read, cheered, and rejected it. Despite this setback, neither producer nor author lost faith in the project. Scenarist Lajos Biro was called in and, with the aid of Korda's staff, as well as contributions from the producer himself, an acceptable, producible script was created.

It is not surprising that a writer of Wells' prestige and stature was distressed to find his original concept edited and reedited many times over before the emergence of a finished product. Through the years it has been reported that Wells was disenchanted with the final screenplay. This may or may not be true, but Wells did go on to script *The Man Who Could Work Miracles* (1937) for Korda. And in commentary from the book version of *Things to Come,* it is apparent that Wells garnered a great deal of satisfaction from seeing his literary efforts integrated with music, costumes, sets, and cinematography.

The problem of the script well under control, Korda next concerned himself with finding the right technical people to handle the production of *Things to Come.* At one point, Korda committed himself to hiring American director Lewis Milestone for the project; Milestone, however, chose instead to direct *Mutiny on the Bounty* for MGM in 1935. After much research and thought, the man ultimately chosen to direct *Things to Come* was William Cameron Menzies.

Born in Scotland, Menzies grew up in the United States and studied art. He entered film as an art director, moving later to overall directing. One of the early films on which he worked in a minor capacity was the Douglas Fairbanks *Thief of Bagdad.* Some years later, he would direct the Korda remake of that silent classic. Menzies had that sense of epic scope, combined with a skill for cutting budgetary corners without sacrificing artistic merit, that were to be requisite for *Things to Come.* Together, he, Korda, and Wells brought *Things to Come* to poetic and beautiful life.

From a purely technical standpoint, *Things to Come* required vistas of ruination as well as depictions of ultra-modern architecture and machinery. It was apparent from the first that great demands would be placed on Korda's special effects department. Realistic-appearing miniature models and sets would be needed, and the task of creating the scale models fell to the great American technician Ned Mann. Mann, not unlike such men as Howard and Theodore Lyedecker, who built the miniatures for the Republic serials and early Irwin Allen television series, worked by one guiding principle—his miniatures would always be built sufficiently large to allow their being photographed from every

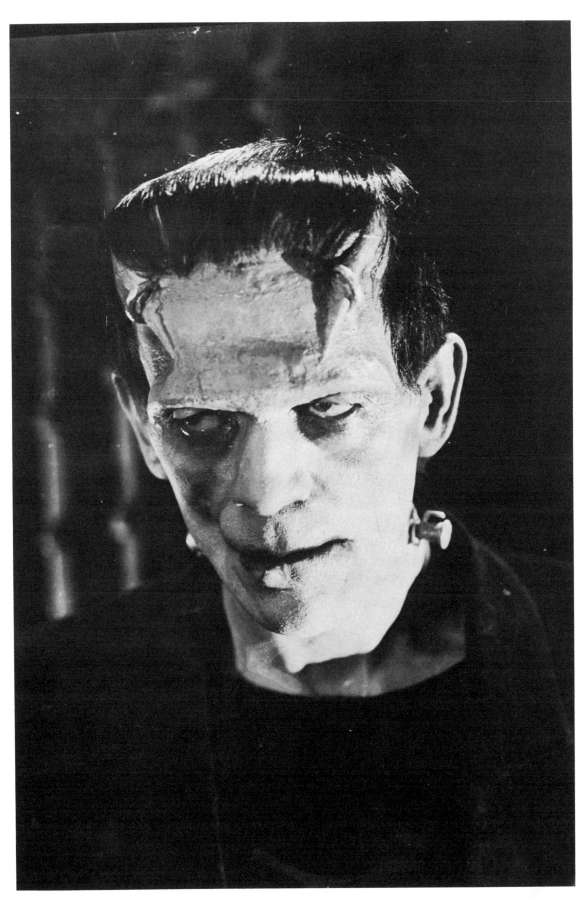

Boris Karloff in the unused trial-makeup for Frankenstein. *The forehead bolts were removed in the final version.*

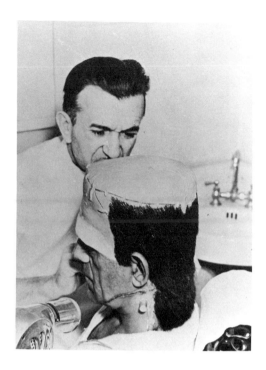

Jack Pierce adds hair to Boris Karloff . This, midway through the laborious four-hour makeup application for Son of Frankenstein.

Boris Karloff takes a cigarette break between takes on set for Bride of Frankenstein.

conceivable angle and distance. This approach melded beautifully with Menzies' own style, which frequently included large-scale panoramic shots.

Mann had perfected his technique of building over many years. He had begun working with miniatures at RKO, and for their production of Deluge (footage of which can be seen in Republic's King of the Rocketmen serial), Mann constructed the New York City skyline in miniature, a set subsequently engulfed by a special-effects tidal wave. However, Korda was most likely drawn to Mann's work as a result of Mann's participation in early Cecil B. DeMille productions such as Madam Satan (1930). In fact, it was doubtless Mann who, later, constructed the incredible miniature soldiers for long-distance shots in DeMille's epic The Crusades, in which conveyor belts and timed mechanisms made entire rows of model soldiers seem to march forward, swaying to and fro.

Boris Karloff explains his remarkable light machine to a stunned audience in The Invisible Ray.

Mann's magnificent miniatures were combined with live actors in the finished film through the talents of another film artist, Harry Zech. Zech had been working in special effects since the earliest days of film. In fact, he was the originator of the first split-screen effect.[2] In *Things to Come,* Zech's split-screen technique was refined to a meticulous art.

The miniatures required of Mann ranged from the familiar to the fantastic. The city of Everytown could have been London, except that during the opening sequences it would be reduced to rubble. Props such as biplanes were required, and even these had to be faked, since they would be shown battling with gigantic—and nonexistent—aircraft. There was the huge space gun to be constructed, as well as the terrain surrounding the awesome structure. Additionally, there were ruined cities, hangars for huge batteries of airplanes, and giant digging machines, not to mention a montage sequence that would bridge the gap between 1936 and the future, showing incredible, enormous automated building centers reconstructing ravaged cities.

A weak aspect of *Metropolis*—the fault of technology, and not Lang—had been that the film's incredible miniatures could not be shown together with live actors in a single shot, except through faulty double-exposure techniques. Together, Mann, Zech, and art director Vincent Korda remedied this situation for *Things to Come.* In sequences wherein miniatures figured prominently with performers and full-sized sets, the lower stories of buildings were constructed life-size, and the miniature upper stories were inserted via matte work.[3] In many cases, paintings of buildings were done on glass. Clear glass was left in portions of the paintings so that the camera could see through the glass and photograph performers and full-sized fragments of sets in the distance. The glass was then braced to the camera and the camera so focused that pane and background action were shot simultaneously. The resultant picture appeared as one continuous full-sized exposure. This technique was used a great deal in the thirties, most notably by Willis O'Brien in *King Kong* (1933) and *Last Days of Pompeii* (1935).

Boris Karloff confronts Bela Lugosi (center) and Walter Kingsford with his amazing telescope in The Invisible Ray.

Two views of Boris Karloff fooling with Ken Strickfadden's extraordinary props created for The Mask of Fu Manchu.

Marguerite Churchill and Edmund Gwenn prepare to bring Boris Karloff back to life in The Walking Dead.

Costumers John Armstrong and Réné Hubert, who worked on such Korda spectacles as *The Private Life of Henry VIII* (1933), had never tackled anything like *Things to Come*. Even for the circa-1936 sequences, fashions had to appear just a bit in advance of their real-life counterparts to remove the film ever so slightly from the present. During the transitional scenes from 1936 to 2036, these same fine fashions had to become moldering, shredded rags. And finally, there were the elaborately mounted futuristic clothes.

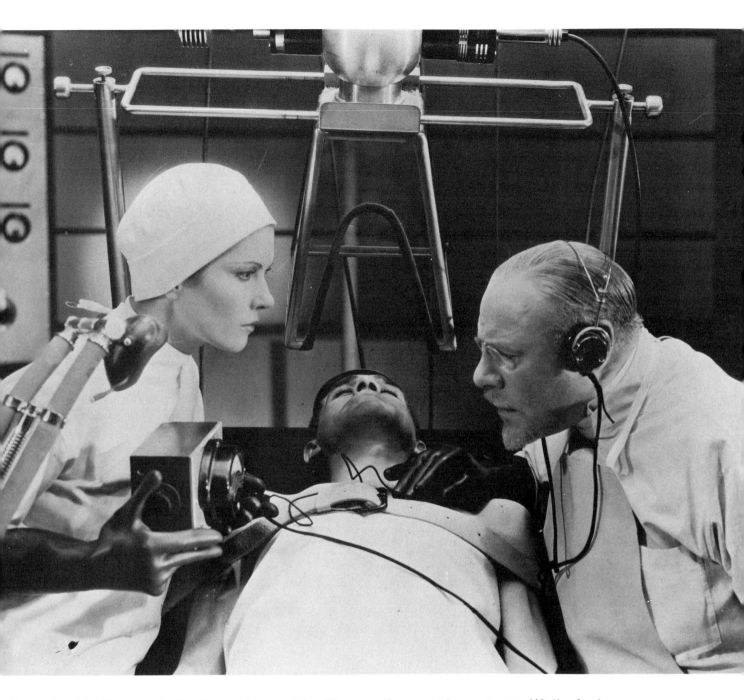

Technical facility aside, the final phase of the film was the most important to Wells, for in this portion would be embodied the sum total of his philosophies and favorable expectations for the future of the human race. Wells wanted to show a world in which machines were the servants of human beings and had allowed man to completely tame his environment.

In the final analysis, the various technical factors fell neatly into their places, and the finished film emerged as a perfectly balanced motion picture. This finesse held true for even the most important post-production facet of the film, the background music, composed by Arthur Bliss. Bliss, who was later knighted and made composer to the queen of England, wrote an individually styled musical background for every sequence in the film.

Rare original ad art for The Walking Dead.

View of Charles Laughton from The Island of Lost Souls.

Charles Laughton, as Dr. Moreau, commands a manimal on The Island of Lost Souls.

Manimals storm the fortress of Dr. Moreau in The Island of Lost Souls.

The exotic Kathleen Burke.

Things to Come opened to rave reviews and was equally honored in Great Britain and the United States. Even in instances where the subject matter was not appreciated, it was acknowledged that *Things to Come* represented techniques of motion-picture production that were as good as, if not better than, anything previously produced in Hollywood. *Things to Come* helped establish Great Britain as a major center of film production.

From the beginning, Wells meant *Things to Come* to be, as he said in the published version of his screenplay, a film of symbolic characters—people who were living embodiments of various personalities and philosophies. For this reason, the characters within the film are solid, hewn of rock, rather than soft and human. They are chess pieces acting a story on a board of Wells's creation, furnishing us with a portrait of the human race shaping a new future after years of fear, indifference, and ignorance. Because of its

A marvelous laboratory from Just Imagine.

John Garrick (left) as J-21, and El Brendel (right) stand beside the ship that will carry them to Mars. From Just Imagine.

professionalism at every turn, *Things to Come* remains an invaluable work to be studied, lest the road to progress be abandoned for a detour into war and social regression.

Less lofty in both scope and philosophy were the great horror films of the thirties. The term *horror*, like *science fiction*, is an amorphous label, and many motion pictures considered horror films contain striking elements of science fiction.

Boris Karloff appeared thrice as the Frankenstein monster—in *Frankenstein* (1931), *Bride of Frankenstein* (1935), and *Son of Frankenstein* (1939), all three of which featured scientific apparatus and electrical sparks galore, as well as the greatest characterization ever by an actor in a horror film, that of Mr. Karloff as the monster.

Karloff struck again as a radioactivated scientist in *The Invisible Ray* (1936), an excellent film wherein Karloff and Bela Lugosi chase down a meteor that landed on earth millions of years before the appearance of human life. With a device of his own invention, Karloff is able to capture light rays from deep space showing earth in prehistoric times, and he witnesses the crash and determines the location of the meteor. Eventually, Karloff locates the space rock, becomes contaminated, and is cursed with a radioactive Midas touch.

The Man Who Lived Again (1936) features Karloff transplanting brains, and *The Man Who Lived Twice* (1936) stars Ralph Bellamy as a criminal whose personality is scientifically altered, allowing him to successfully elude the police. Death rays and scientific apparatus abound in *Mask of Fu Manchu* (1932), with Karloff again in the lead and again under layers of makeup, and the inimitable Karloff is executed and returned to life in *The Walking Dead* (1936), also starring Marguerite Churchill and Warren Hull.

*A meticulously crafted set from
Just Imagine.*

Gloria Stuart receives a gracious
kiss from The Invisible Man.

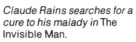

The Invisible Man confronts his
tormentors.

Claude Rains searches for a
cure to his malady in The
Invisible Man.

The Invisible Man steps out for a
drink.

Island of Lost Souls (1933) was another Wells adaptation, this time based on the master's *Island of Dr. Moreau*. The film—dominated by a fine Charles Laughton performance as the evil doctor—features visitors to an island who discover a mad scientist performing experiments on animals, sending them eons ahead in evolution. The result is a horrifying collection of "manimals," animals pushed close to where man now resides on the evolutionary scale. Needless to say, Moreau is destroyed when the manimals revolt, while the hero and his sweetheart escape unscathed.

Just Imagine (1930) is more classical, traditional science fiction wherein, *Metropolis*-like, we get a glimpse of the world of the future. The sets are reminiscent of Lang's work although slightly more sophisticated, but the film hasn't *Metropolis'* class or striking thematic thread. And then, with horror overtones, there is the timeless adaptation of another Wells work, *The Invisible Man* (1933), marking the screen debut of two major film forces. One was the late Claude Rains, who here began a distinguished career that included such films as the Oscar-winning *Phantom of the Opera* (1943) and *Lawrence of Arabia* (1962). The other force was the magnificent *Invisible Man* special effects of John P.

Publicity still showing Fredric March in his Oscar-winning portrayal as Dr. Jekyll and Mr. Hyde.

Fulton, effects illustrated when the title character unwraps his bandaged body to reveal emptiness therein. These effects would reappear in such films as *The Invisible Man Returns, The Invisible Man's Revenge,* and *Abbott and Costello Meet the Invisible Man,* all in the forties.

Strictly *science* fiction is the spectacular *Transatlantic Tunnel* (1935), an interesting, technically creditable film of an undersea commuter rail between the United States and Europe. With emphasis on horror, there was *Dr. X* (1932), featuring Preston Foster as a mad scientist–murderer with one arm who discovers a synthetic flesh and creates a new limb.

Another mad-doctor film, *Dr. Jekyll and Mr. Hyde* (1932), earned Fredric March an Oscar for his striking performance as Robert Lewis Stevenson's infamous dabbler in the human psyche. Remakes of *Dr. Jekyll and Mr. Hyde* featuring Spencer Tracy (1941) and Ralph Bates (in the 1972 *Dr. Jekyll and Sister Hyde*) never came close to the March version.

Miriam Hopkins is all choked up in *Dr. Jekyll and Mr. Hyde.*

Buster Crabbe and Jean Rogers on a staircase from Bride of Frankenstein, *here a setting on the planet Mongo for* Flash Gordon.

35

Ada Ince and one of the mechanical men from The Vanishing Shadow.

Charles Middleton, as Ming the Merciless, and entourage from Flash Gordon.

"Lightning" plans to subjugate the world from on board his atmospheric craft. From Fighting Devil Dogs.

Analyses of what made serials so popular have been created and re-created by scores of pseudo-intellectuals. Hypotheses range from the sound to the ridiculous and parallel theorems explaining why comic-book sales were awesome in the forties. Coincidentally, both were popular at the same time. Indeed, from comic books came many serial plots and characters, such as Captain Marvel, Batman, Captain America, and

Buster Crabbe in a publicity still for Flash Gordon's Trip to Mars.

Buster Crabbe in dress blues from Flash Gordon Conquers the Universe.

Superman, and the serial medium has often been labeled the cinema comic book, with its continued-next-week format, simple narrative style, and superhuman personnel.

Untouched by comics or cliché were early serials such as *The Vanishing Shadow* (1934), featuring death rays and radio-controlled robots, and *Fighting Devil Dogs* (1938), featuring an ominously garbed criminal named Lightning who fired lightning bolts at his adversaries and zipped through the stratosphere in a sleek-looking plane known as the Wing.

Another screen adventure came from a comic *strip* and proved both the most popular and the most expensive (budgeted at an unheard-of $350,000) serial of all time. This was *Flash Gordon.* Despite the lofty price tag—more than double that of most serial films—its

Buster Crabbe prepares for flight in Buck Rogers.

37

The original ad art for the feature version of the Buck Rogers *serial.*

The original ad art for Undersea Kingdom.

sets and music were lifted from the 1933 *Bride of Frankenstein.* But the 1936 film boasts elaborate production values, some fancy special effects, and, of course, the marvelous personification of Flash by Buster Crabbe.

The plot is simple. Flash, Dr. Zarkov, and romantic interest Dale Arden take to space in Dr. Zarkov's untested spaceship and journey to the planet Mongo to save Earth from eruptions being caused by Ming the Merciless, the mad emperor of Mongo. Needless to say, our hero succeeds in putting Ming out of commission for the nonce, ignorant that he and the emperor will butt horns again in films to come.

As Flash, Crabbe is sincere and bears a striking resemblance to the comic character. As Dale, Jean Rogers is properly attractive and supplies someone after whom Ming can lust.

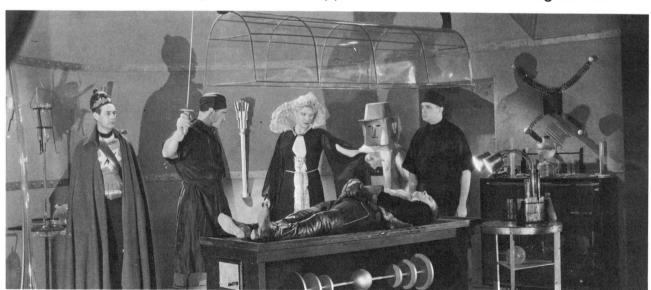

Dorothy Christy, as Queen Tika, prepares to bring Gene Autry back to life in Phantom Empire.

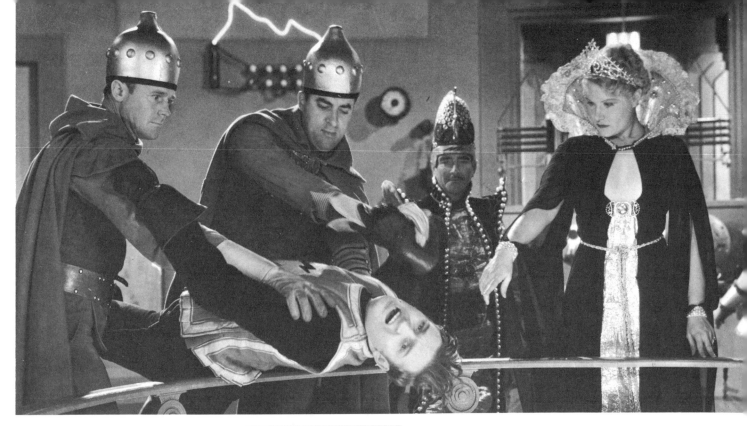

Gene Autry in various stages of peril, a prisoner of The Phantom Empire.

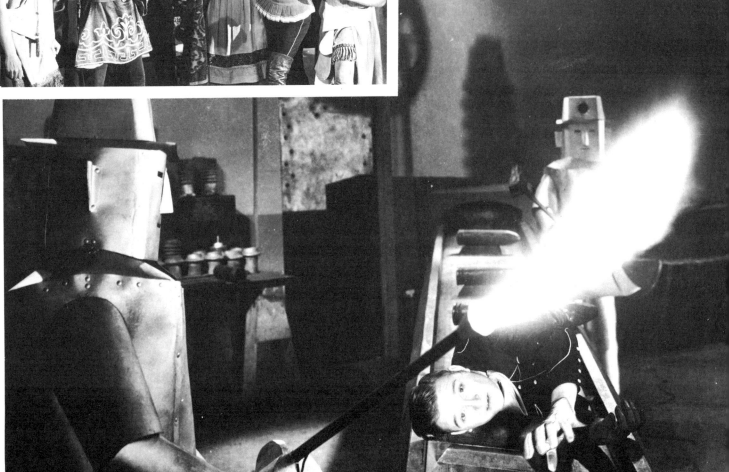

Bela Lugosi's murderous robot goes through his paces in Phantom Creeps.

᠎Copperhead battles The Mysterious Dr. Satan's deadly robot.

Two views of the Purple Monster (Roy Barcroft) from The Purple Monster Strikes.

William Boyd has Claudia Dell right where he wants her in the 1935 serial The Lost City. Boyd, as Zolok, hopes to cripple the world into submission via death rays, zombies, and such. He is foiled by Kane Richmond of Spy Smasher fame.

Judd Holdren in Zombies of the Stratosphere, *the feature version of which became* Satan's Satellites.

Roy Barcroft, as Retik, nemesis to Commando Cody in Radar Men From the Moon.

Zarkov, portrayed by Frank Shannon, is properly sage and learned in his role, and of course, Charles Middleton's Ming is superb.

Middleton was the perfect movie villain—royal, menacing, and ruthless. He was so ruthless, in fact, that after his death in *Flash Gordon,* Ming returned to menace our hero—with no explanation of his resurrection—in 1938, in *Flash Gordon's Trip to Mars.* This film had a greater emphasis on gadgetry than the original, but all the elements of entertainment were there.

A final Flash Gordon serial, *Flash Gordon Conquers the Universe,* was released in 1939, but by this time the formula had worn thin. Changing Dale from Jean Rogers to Carol Hughes was hardly beneficial, and the plot—Ming's infecting earth with the Purple Death—wasn't at all worthy of the characters' potential.

Yet, despite whatever failings the adventures had, an amazing element was the great variety of creatures Flash faced and overcame. Lionmen, Sharkmen, Treemen, undulating masses of living clay, Hawkmen, Orangopods, Tigrons, and Ostosacs—not to mention Rockmen—menaced our hero at one time or another during the trilogy.[4]

Buster Crabbe returned in the title role of *Buck Rogers* (1939), a serial based on Phillip Nowlan's fantastic novel *Armageddon: 2419 A.D.,* the plot of which finds our hero put to sleep for five hundred years by Nirvano gas, only to be awakened from timeless repose by the menace of Killer Kane and the Zuggs of Saturn.

Yet another film featuring science fiction as a major component was *Phantom Empire,* the 1935 Gene Autry film wherein our hero finds, in a remote corner of his vast ranch, an entrance to Murania, a scientific paradise twenty-five thousand feet below the surface of the earth, ruled by Queen Tika. Gene helps her overcome the traitorous Lord Argo, and

A still from Lost Planet Airmen, the feature version of King of the Rocketmen. Pictured are Mae Clarke and Tris Coffin.

George Wallace as Commando Cody in Radar Men From the Moon.

she revives Autry when he is killed—a dubious exchange at best. The film was directed by the talented team of Otto Brower and B. Reeves Eason, two of the finest second-unit directors in film history.[5]

Undersea Kingdom is a 1936 serial of the *Phantom Empire* school featuring Ray "Crash" Corrigan (who in 1958 would play the monster martian in *It! The Terror from Beyond Space*) as a marine who accompanies a scientific expedition to the bottom of the sea, where they find the kingdom of Atlantis and its futuristic scientific wizardry. Their arrival comes none to soon, for the Atlanteans are preparing to invade the surface world with ray guns and robots known as Volkites. One noteworthy asset of *Undersea Kingdom* was the casting of Lane Chandler and Lon Chaney, Jr.—famous for Westerns and horror films, respectively—as Black Robe henchmen of Unga Khan, the notorious Atlantean leader.

Moving from Atlantis to the surface world, we find the great Bela Lugosi hard at work as evil Dr. Alex Zorka in the 1939 film *Phantom Creeps.* In this effort, Lugosi finds a meteor (in stock-footage sequences from *The Invisible Ray*) that gives him the power to put people to sleep. With the aid of an enormous robot and a belt of invisibility, Lugosi and his criminal assistant, Monk, essay to conquer the world. They are thwarted by the good Dr. Mallory.

Dave Sharpe, the stunt actor/double for Tris Coffin, in King of the Rocketmen.

The Mysterious Dr. Satan (1940) features Eduardo Cianelli and his murderous giant robot at odds with the Copperhead, a hooded do-gooder, while from Mars, *The Purple Monster Strikes* (1945) in the person of Roy Bancroft. In this minor effort, our Purple Monster Martian has the power to make himself invisible and enter the bodies of Earthlings he has killed.

Back in space, on *The Lost Planet* (1953), a very dapper Dr. Grood has enslaved Earthlings on the planet Ergro to mine cosmonium, a metal that creates a deadly ray when mixed with dornite. This potential disaster followed closely on the heels of a 1951 visit from the *Flying Disc Man from Mars,* a character named Mota who lands in a volcano that erupts after a dozen chapters, sending Mota and his saucer back to Mars in many scattered fragments.

Radar Men from the Moon (1952) featured Clayton Moore, TV's Lone Ranger, in a minor role, and George Wallace as Commando Cody, the rocket-powered, helmeted superhero fighting Retik the Ruler, who visits Earth to conquer it with his lunarium ray.

Dick Purcell, as Captain America, *flattens a wrongdoer.*

Meanwhile, from only as far as out as Earth's atmosphere came *Zombies of the Stratosphere,* a 1952 disaster that features, for completists, the robot first used in *The Mysterious Dr. Satan,* as well as Leonard Nimoy as an invader fifteen years before he became *Star Trek*'s Mr. Spock. *Commando Cody* (1953) pitted the jet-age hero against an invader from Mercury, and it was up to our northern neighbors to save the United States from foreign agents in *The Canadian Mounties vs. the Atomic Invaders* (1953). *Captain Video* hit the serial circuit in 1951 to do battle with Vultura of Atoma. An uneasy mixing of the old and the new was released in 1951: Rulu, a lovely lady from Mercury, journeyed to Captain Nemo's *Mysterious Island* in search of a radioactive metal with which to destroy Earth. The film was not a bad idea; unfortunately, it missed the boat . . . but not, alas, the planet.

Tom Tyler as The Phantom,
based on Lee Falk's classic
comic strip.

George Reeves as
Superman.

King of the Rocket Men was a 1949 predecessor of Commando Cody—both were jet-propelled crime fighters. From the planet Krypton in 1948 came the durable *Superman,* played by Kirk Alyn. In this film, the man of steel did battle with the Spider Lady and her reducer ray; in the sequel *Atom Man vs. Superman,* the superhero was in more familiar comic-book territory fighting his long-time archenemy Lex Luthor. In *Superman and the Mole Men* (1951), a feature-film starring George Reeves, who went on to play the role for television, tiny creatures crawl from the world's deepest oil well with their ray guns, to menace a small Midwestern town. Superman rights everything, though. The creatures were only protecting their home and, as is just, the oil well is shut down.

Superman's comic-book blood brother Batman met with a scientific menace known as Dr. Daka, played by J. Carroll Naish, in *Batman* (1943), in which Naish was able to control people's minds with his nefarious scientific wizardry. The serials did nothing more to advance and mature cinema science fiction than did the comic book to advance fantastic literature. But they were fun, escapist fare, and without sophistication, they gave an audience more thrills per minute for their money than *Bullitt and The French Connection* combined. And in the forties and fifties, serials plus thrills equaled box office.

The Forties

Boris Karloff very much preoccupied with demonic experiments in The Devil Commands.

Boris Karloff (right) makes new and terrifying discoveries in the realm of life and death. From The Man They Could Not Hang.

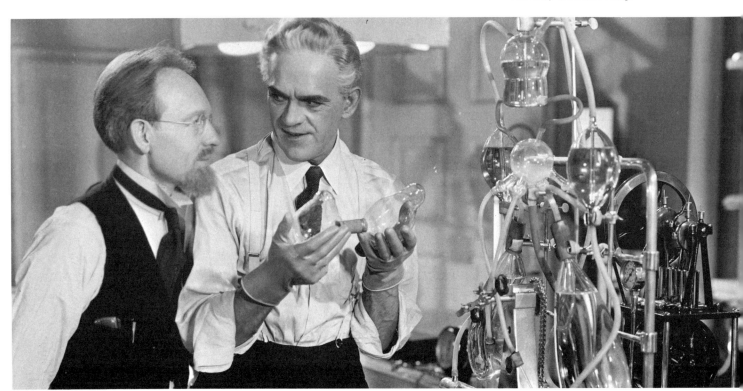

Aside from serials, the forties saw very little traditional science fiction. Hollywood, especially, was still in the throes of the horror cycle. Yet, horror in the forties was no longer solely supernatural or of strictly satanic origins, as had been films such as *Cabinet of Dr. Caligari* (1919), the Lon Chaney, Sr., films, and *The Mummy* (1932) and *Dracula* (1931). The supernatural did figure in *Wolfman* (1941), with the late Lon Chaney, Jr., and in the Karloff-Lugosi *Body Snatcher* (1945), but Boris Karloff, in the guise of many a mad scientist, paved the way and rode herd on the new breed of scientific horror film begun with *The Invisible Ray* in 1936.

The Man They Could Not Hang (1939)[6] was one of Karloff's early demented-doctor opuses, featuring him as Dr. Henryk Savaard, inventor of an ingenious mechanical heart. Certain that his device will work, Savaard convinces a student to allow himself to be killed so that Karloff can revive him with the artificial heart. But the student's fiancée calls the police after the murder, and they arrest and hang Karloff. Acting resourcefully, Karloff's assistant uses the heart on Boris, and the reborn doctor seeks out and murders those who sentenced him to death.

From left to right: John Shepperd, (later known as Shepperd Strudwick), Lynne Roberts, George Zucco, and the great J. Carrol Naish in Dr. Renault's Secret.

Vincent Price and Nan Grey at the beginning and the end of The Invisible Man Returns.

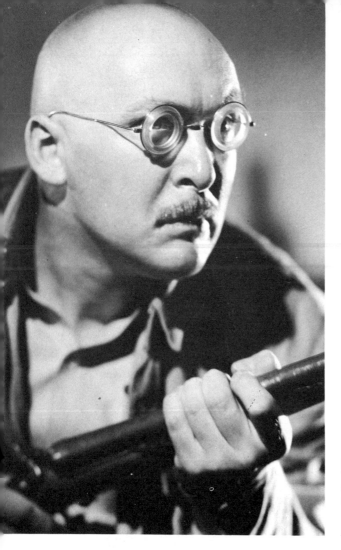

Dr. Cyclops *greets Janice Logan, Thomas Coley, Charles Halton, and Victor Kilian before shrinking them to six inches in height.*

Albert Dekker as the mad Dr. Cyclops.

The Man They Could Not Hang was followed by *The Man With Nine Lives* (1940), in which Karloff, as Dr. Leon Kravaal, works to cure cancer by freezing his patients. *Before I Hang* (1941) was next, with Karloff again killing a man, this time asserting that he has found a cure for death. About to be hanged for this murder, Karloff injects himself with the antideath serum, manufactured with the blood of a hanged convict, but as fate would have it, Karloff is granted a reprieve. He starts killing people on the slightest provocation—the influence of the killer's blood—and is finally shot to death by a policeman.

Finally, in 1941, came *The Devil Commands,* the last of the forties mad-scientist films for Karloff. In this movie Karloff invents a machine that records brain waves on a graph. Hoping to use the machine to communicate with his newly dead wife, Karloff experiments on human guinea pigs and in the process either renders them dumb or kills them. When the facility is blown sky high, Karloff is buried beneath the debris.

J. Carroll Naish was an ape turned human by George Zucco in *Dr. Renault's Secret* (1942), in which Naish turns in a creditable and highly sympathetic performance as an ape man who is more human than his mentor.

The Invisible Man Returns (1940), with Vincent Price in the fore, and *The Invisible Man's Revenge* (1944) played in theaters across the country. In the first film Price is a man on

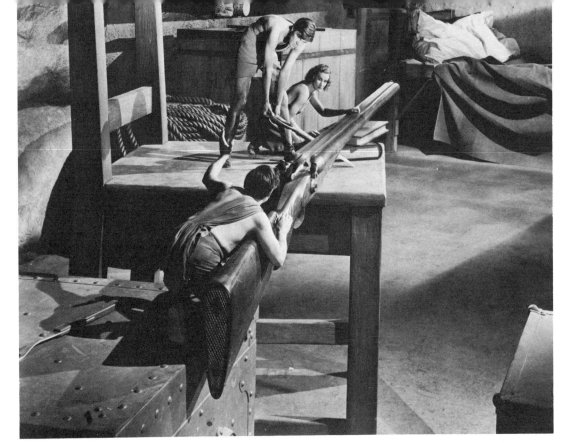

A look at the incredible props for the amazing film version of Dr. Cyclops.

*Moments before his fatal plunge
into the well, Dr. Cyclops
searches for his shrunken guests.*

death row who quaffs his brother's invisibility serum after a friend had the potion
smuggled into jail. Once free, Price clears himself of the murder rap. *The Invisible Man's
Revenge* featured Jon Hall as the amazing transparent man, but by now the series had
bogged down in mediocrity.

Lon Chaney, Jr., as the
electrically charged Man-Made
Monster.

Glenn Strange as the man-made
werewolf in Mad Monster.

John Barrymore, a phantom
Virginia Bruce, and Donald
MacBride in The Invisible
Woman.

Bela Lugosi as the genetically restructured Ape Man.

One of the first great science-fiction epics of American film was the 1940 effort *Dr. Cyclops. Dr. Cyclops* is the story of a scientist who, using atomic rays in his Peruvian-jungle hideaway, shrinks several people to doll size. The sets and special effects are top notch, as are the performances by all concerned. Regrettably, the situations contrived for the shrunken characters could have been more inventive. It's difficult to imagine being more frightened of an angry crocodile at six inches than at six feet; it would have been better had director Ernest Shoedsack given the victims problems and situations unique to their height. But the film is a good one, a work of great drama as the beleaguered characters match wits with the sadistic, near-blind scientist.

An undistinguished potpourri of horror-science-fiction films was made during the forties, and a random sampling reveals *The Mad Monster* (1942), starring Glenn Strange as a

Onslow Stevens (as the mad doctor) and Glenn Strange in House of Dracula.

54

Lon Chaney, Jr., as the monster in Ghost of Frankenstein.

Glenn Strange and Lon Chaney Jr., as the wolfman, menace our heroes in Abbott and Costello Meet Frankenstein.

55

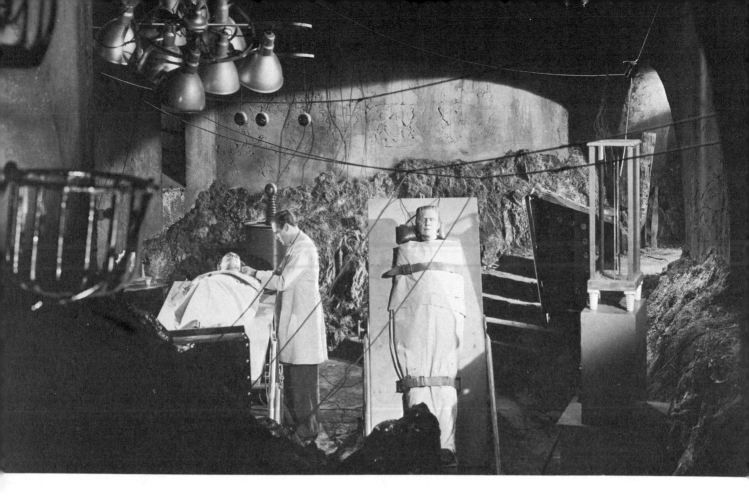

hairy beast; *The Invisible Woman* (1941), a silly tongue-in-cheek effort the title of which says it all; *The Ape Man* (1943), wherein Bela Lugosi seeks scientific means to duplicate, chemically, the strength of an ape; *Captive Wild Woman* (1943), nothing more than an ape female transformed surgically from simian to human; and Lon Chaney, Jr., as a dead truck driver brought back to life by Lionel Atwill and a large dose of electricity in *Man-Made Monster* (1941).

House of Frankenstein (1945), *Ghost of Frankenstein* (1942), and *Frankenstein Meets the Wolfman* (1943) brought back Mary Shelley's electric-born monster to the screen. *House of Frankenstein* and *Ghost of Frankenstein* gave the monster role to Glenn Strange and Lon Chaney, Jr., respecitvely, and in *Frankstein Meets the Wolfman* a dreadfully miscast Bela Lugosi wore the monster makeup. The monster also made a guest appearance in *House of Dracula* (1945), with Strange doing the honors.

Abbott and Costello met up with Frankenstein, Wolfman, Dracula, and the Invisible Man in *Abbott and Costello Meet Frankenstein* (1948); with a boxer gone invisible to clear himself of his trainer's murder in *Abbott and Costello Meet the Invisible Man* (1951); and with Boris Karloff as the infamous doctor in *Abbott and Costello Meet Dr. Jekyll and Mr. Hyde* (1953).

So ended the forties. Now George Pal and Ray Harryhausen would give science fiction its biggest shot in the arm since Georges Méliès. What followed was a dramatic snowballing of the genre, a growth unique in film history—and as it had been with Méliès, a trip to the moon was the catalyst.

Patrick Knowles prepares for some bizarre experimentation in Frankenstein Meets the Wolfman. *It is in this lab the mortsters have their grand finale slug-fest.*

Glenn Strange (left) and Bela Lugosi (right) between takes on Abbott and Costello Meet Frankenstein.

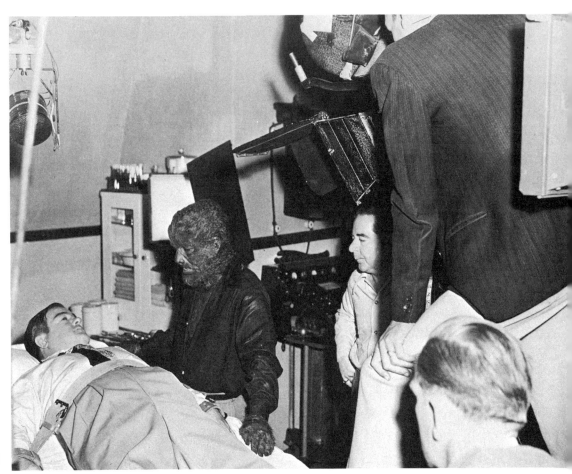

Behind the scenes on Abbott and Costello Meet Frankenstein.

The Fifties

The Beast from Twenty Thousand Fathoms *goes on a rampage of destruction through the streets of New York.*

The Beast from Twenty Thousand Fathoms *is trapped inside a Coney Island roller coaster, where he is shot to death with a radioactive isotope.*

Setting up the sound stage for an Arctic sequence in Beast from Twenty Thousand Fathoms.

The fifties opened with a bang, featuring back-to-back hits in *Rocketship XM* and *Destination Moon*. Science fiction became big box office, and the decade that followed saw a fantastic diversity in quality, scope, subject matter, and acceptance on many different levels for the science-fiction film.

For the most part, science-fiction pictures during this period were an unpretentious, novel, and exciting lot, and even though some were quick, sloppy, and of dubious intent, they were all fun, entertaining films. Perhaps to look back on them with nostalgia, rather than

Paula Raymond, Paul Christian, Jack Pennick, and Cecil Kellaway examine a sketch of The Beast from Twenty Thousand Fathoms. *Pennick is one of the two survivors of a ship wrecked by the monster.*

with a cool critical eye, is unprofessional. Yet in these pre-moon-landing, pre-sixties films, unrestricted by political and technological sophistication, imaginations ran free and rampant.

Giants, ogres, and king-sized animals have been part of human culture since biblical times. From David and Goliath, to Beowulf, to the present time, our visual arts and literature have shown a marked propensity for the gargantuan. It comes as no surprise, then, that monsters were huge in the fifties, as was catastrophe on a galactic scale. Insects grew to monstrous heights, reptiles from prehistory returned to ravage the world, and all manner of atomic mutations greeted theatergoers. People flocked to see flying saucers, mass destruction, death on a grand scale, and similar science-based threats. Truly, all forms of plausible menace saw the light of the silver screen during this period.

A publicity still from Rodan.

The twin Rodan *monsters go winging from their mountain hideaway.*

The mighty city of Tokyo falls before the onslaught of Rodan.

In the world's deepest mine shaft, Rodan *hatches from centuries of hibernation.*

Gigantis, the Fire Monster *(right)*
prepares to do battle with Anzilla.

MONSTERS ON THE LOOSE

The atom bomb was responsible for resurrecting many and varied forms of prehistoric fauna, and a superb film of this type is Ray Harryhausen's *Beast from Twenty Thousand Fathoms* (1953). Nuclear tests in the North Pole free a rhedosaurus (a fictional monster that is part brontosaurus, part tyrannosaurus) from icy hibernation. The Beast makes for the Hudson River in New York City, the basin of which is the monster's ancestral breeding ground, leaving death and carnage in his wake. Cornered in an amusement park, the monster is killed by a radioactive isotope shot from a rifle wielded by a then unknown Lee van Cleef. Scenes of devastation, such as the destruction of a lighthouse done entirely in silhouette, are eerie and flawlessly executed. The climax, with the monster amok at Coney

*San Francisco quakes and falls
before the titanic tentacles of* It
Came from Beneath the Sea.

The Golden Gate Bridge is just one of the many San Franciscan landmarks to feel the might of It Came from Beneath the Sea.

Island, is breathtaking. The film moves quickly, and the fact that there is a monster loose in New York is taken very matter-of-factly by all concerned. The acting—especially that of Cecil Kellaway as a lovable paleontologist who is killed by the Beast midway through the film—is good, the directing restrained, and the film both entertaining and intelligent.

Not wishing to find themselves in the midst of a dinosaur (ergo box-office) gap, the Japanese entered the reptile race in 1955 with an amphibious hybrid monster known as *Godzilla, King of the Monsters,* a fire-breathing tyrannosaurus with stegosaurian back plates. Called, in Japan, "Gojira," Godzilla is awakened by hydrogen-bomb tests and, with not quite the same logic behind his moves as the Beast from Twenty Thousand Fathoms, makes for Tokyo and levels it. Although added scenes, filmed in the United States with Raymond Burr, intercut very badly with the original Japanese print, *Godzilla* is a magnificent technical achievement. Substituting a man in a monster suit and mechanical models for Ray Harryhausen's frame-at-a-time animated creations, special-effects man Eiji Tsuburaya destroyed the Japanese metropolis with alarming realism. And although the twenty-story-tall creature was done in by Dr. Serizawa's oxygen destroyer, the durable dinosaur would return for no fewer than a dozen sequels, the latest of which, *Godzilla vs. the Smog Monster* (1971), features Godzilla as a good guy.

Another Japanese monster of great impact made its debut in 1957—*Rodan, the Flying Monster.* The monsters Rodan—a pair of enormous pteronodons—hatch from long-buried

A peek at the amphibious killer called The Monster from Piedras Blancas.

The sub-oceanic caterpillar known as The Monster That Challenged the World.

eggs locked deep within the bowels of a dormant volcano and rise up to devastate Japan. The terrifying pterodactyls are eventually destroyed by lava released upon their mountain lair by a barrage of army rockets. But old monsters never die. Rodan, like Godzilla, returned throughout the sixties and seventies and proved to be one of Japan's greatest box-office stars.

Released in the United States with *Rodan* was an adequate effort known as *Gigantis, the Fire Monster*, in reality a sequel—the first—to *Godzilla* wherein the radioactive creature returns from the dead to do battle with a porcupine-like reptile known as Anzilla (who, though defeated in this film, returned with Godzilla and Rodan in later monster epics).

In 1955 Ray Harryhausen brought us an enormous five-tentacled octopus in *It Came from Beneath the Sea*. Though not as cogent as *Beast from Twenty Thousand Fathoms*, this film has many assets, most of them, not surprisingly, of a technical nature. The destruction of the Golden Gate Bridge, the sinking of a ship at sea, and the monster's death by torpedo are most impressive, and the battle between soldiers bearing flame throwers and the octopus is a sight to behold.

Also from the sea came *The Monster That Challenged the World* (1957), a prehistoric caterpillar; *The Attack of the Crab Monsters* (1957), artificially enlarged crustaceans that menace a small party stranded on a remote island; *Phantom from Ten Thousand Leagues* (1955), a man-sized, scale-encrusted fish being that serves as a barely diverting subplot

63

The Creature from the Black Lagoon *prepares to attack an intruder to his Amazonian domain: Man!*

A drugged Gill Man floats helplessly in his water-logged prison. From Revenge of the Creature.

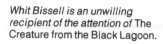

Whit Bissell is an unwilling recipient of the attention of The Creature from the Black Lagoon.

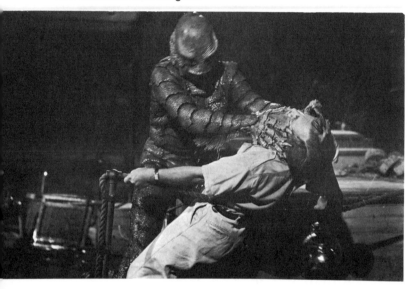

The Creature from the Black Lagoon *makes a pass at a none-too-happy Julia Adams.*

Gill Man is given air by Rex Reason.

The Giant Behemoth, *in the film of the same name, rises from the Thames.*

to a routine murder mystery; the gumdrop-shaped *Monster from the Ocean Floor* (1957); the brutal Mexican *Monster from Piedras Blancas* (1954); and of course, *The Creature from the Black Lagoon* (1954). The Creature from the Black Lagoon is an amphibious being that lurks beneath the murky waters of the Amazon River. Theorized to be a creature born of amphibian evolution that has run parallel to that of man, the lagoon lord is captured, takes a liking to Julie Adams, and is harpooned to death. Or so it seemed—but a year later we were treated to the *Revenge of the Creature* and, in 1956, *The Creature Walks Among Us.* An interesting departure from the mundane was undertaken by the third film of the series, in which the Creature is given plastic surgery and made to look more human; however, he is dissatisfied with the life of a surface dweller and, after much to-do, returns to the sea.

The last of the major prehistoric monsters on the loose of the fifties was Willis O'Brien's *Giant Behemoth* (1958). Not up to Mr. O'Brien's *King Kong* (1933) or, for that matter, any of his student Harryhausen's work in the fifties, *Giant Behemoth* does have excellent performances by Gene Evans (one of the most underrated talents in film) and André Morell, as well as atmospheric, well-paced direction by Eugene Lourie, the director responsible for *Beast from Twenty Thousand Fathoms.* The special effects are alternately good and bad. Scenes of the monster marching through city streets charring people with his radioactive rays are convincing; not as effective are shots of a stiff papier-mâché monster head that attacks a ferry boat in the Thames and pops up from time to time in very miniaturish and silly-looking sets. The script is fairly literate, and the film has some striking London location photography. With a larger budget, it could have been the equal of Mr. Lourie's earlier monster effort.

Giant bugs were extremely popular in the fifties, and the epitome of the big-bug stories was *Them!* (1954), wherein giant ants invade the sewers of Los Angeles. The creatures are eventually burned to a crisp by flame throwers, but not before they crush the life from star James Whitmore. The film is well acted and suspenseful, and although it is slightly contrived and melodramatic, it holds up well today.

The Giant Behemoth *marches through London, destroying all in his path.*

James Whitmore looks on as
Edmund Gwenn explains the
intricacies of ant-life to
authorities. James Arness and
Joan Weldon (seated), however,
have eyes only for each other.
From Them!

One of the radioactivated
monster ants emerges from his
desert dwelling in Them!

James Arness and Joan Weldon
at the mercy of a monster ant in
Them!

James Whitmore (left), James
Arness, and Joan Weldon
examine the gassed remains of
Them! Unfortunately, a fecund
queen ant has escaped.

A publicity still from Them!
Shown are James Arness and
Joan Weldon.

A close-up publicity still showing one of the models used in The Tarantula.

Not quite as good as *Them!* was the 1955 effort *The Tarantula,* a better-than-average bug-monster flick with Leo G. Carroll as a mad scientist responsible for fostering the monstrous arachnid. (As an insect-aside, like the ants in *Them!,* the spider-giant is fried to death by an aerial flame bomb.)

Less memorable on all counts was the ridiculously embarrassing *Deadly Mantis* (1957). Once again, a monster heads from the Arctic to warmer climes, this time, however, to the

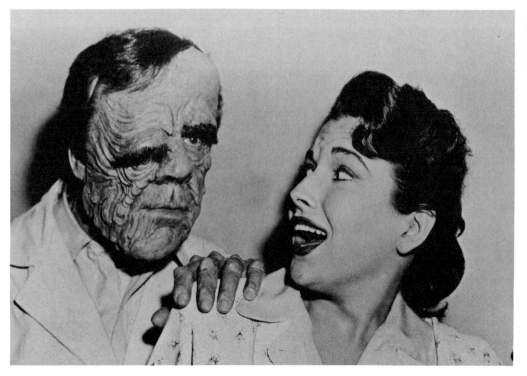

Leo G. Carroll has been transformed into a monster by injecting himself with a special formula of his own concoction. From The Tarantula.

accompaniment of awful Clifford Stine special effects. The creature's death in New York's Holland Tunnel is laughable. Willis O'Brien presented the Mexican populace with a *Black Scorpion* (1957), the title monster of which headed a herd of animated insects loosed from the earth's core by volcanic action, while animated wasps grown giant from exposure to solar rays were the featured creatures in *Monster from Green Hell* (1957).

Bugs enlarged by cosmic rays were the main attraction in *Cosmic Monsters* (1958), a film with nary a claim to fame save for the presence of star Forrest Tucker. Better—but not by much—was Bert I. Gordon's *Beginning of the End* (1957), starring Peter Graves, who had the impossible mission of ridding Chicago of monster grasshoppers. Why he didn't simply borrow the Deadly Mantis is quizzical. The film's technical effects are better than Gordon's usual, and the same can be said for the acting and directing. One particularly well-done sequence is the first appearance of the bugs, when they attack and devour a mute scientist. The portrait of the doomed man mouthing a scream that never comes is both frightening and effective.

Bert Gordon also spearheaded the attack in *Earth vs. the Spider* (1958), when the latter is discovered lurking in a cave (and is subsequently captured, thought dead, revives, breaks loose, ravages a small town, and murders indiscriminantly by sucking all the blood from its victims). The Spider, once cornered in his lair, is electrocuted.

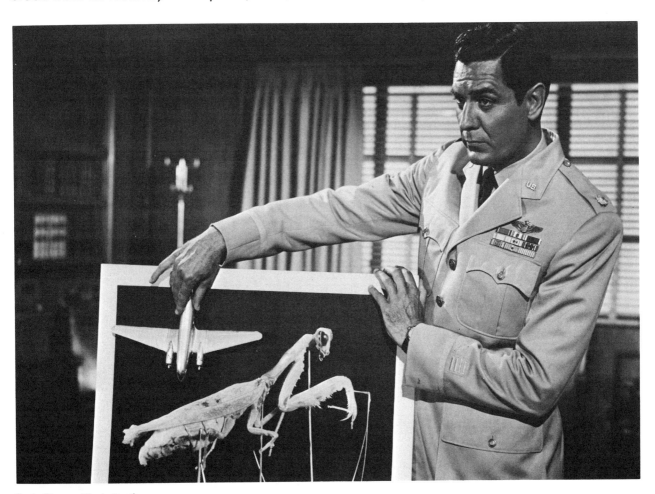

Craig Stevens illustrates the relative size of The Deadly Mantis.

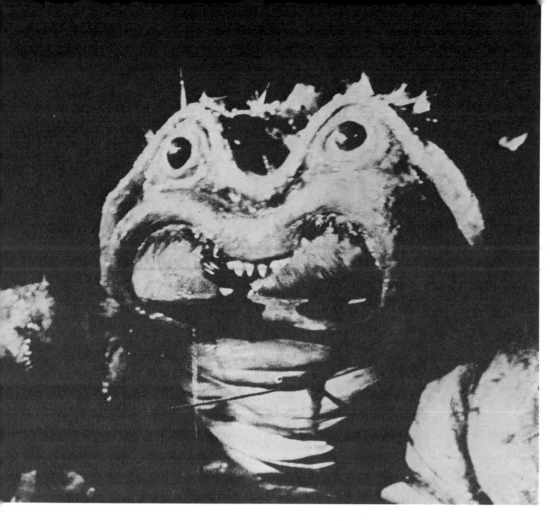

A close-up of the life-size model used in The Black Scorpion.

The only bugs in *The Giant Gila Monster* (1959) were of a technical nature as teenagers sought to rid the world of one of the silliest, most dimwitted monsters ever. It's unfortunate that a decade of monsters on the loose, begun so brilliantly by Ray Harryhausen and his *Beast from Twenty Thousand Fathoms,* should close with such a resounding thud.

A pair of natives feel the pinch of The Monster from Green Hell.

Gaby Andre is ensnared by one of the awesome bugs known as The Cosmic Monsters.

bug's-eye view of Patricia Owens as she sees her husband, or the first time, as The Fly.

MEN INTO MONSTERS

Radiation is again responsible for a major monster in *The Amazing Colossal Man* (1957). Attempting to rescue the pilot of a plane crashed on the test site of the world's first plutonium-bomb blast, Glenn Langan is caught in the explosion. Charred from head to toe, the soldier heals and promptly starts to grow, several feet every day. Understandably, his mind starts to slip, and he goes on a rampage of Las Vegas, ripping out miniature trees, lifting toy cars, and making a general pest of himself.

In one hilarious sequence, two men attempt to give the giant an injection with an enormous hypodermic needle. They stick him in the heel; he removes the needle and proceeds to skewer one of the men on it. (Had the giant been named Achilles, some deeper significance might have been read into this scene.) After much to-do, the Colossal

The scientifically mutated beings known as The Alligator People *in various stages of development.*

71

Forrest Tucker (center) is somewhat befuddled by the dazed look of an outer space visitor in Cosmic Monsters.

Man is shot from Boulder Dam and perishes—until the following year, when he returns in the far superior sequel, *War of the Colossal Beast.*

This film opens with a frightened Mexican lad running for his life from something we cannot see. The owner of the truck the boy had been driving contacts the police, and a party goes in search of the vehicle. Along with the dismembered food truck, they find the Colossal Man. Evidently he did not die when shot from the dam; however, his face and shoulder were horribly mutilated by the bazooka blast and his subsequent plunge into the water. Hence, the Colossal *Beast.*

He is captured and bound in a hangar at Los Angeles International Airport, but he escapes and goes on a technically more convincing rampage than in the previous film. After threatening to crack in half a school bus loaded with children, the monster decides to end it all and grabs some high-voltage wires, electrocuting himself.

A third film from director-writer, special-effects man Gordon is not as easily analyzed as his other efforts. If *Attack of the Fifty Foot Woman* (1958) was intended to be taken seriously, it's the worst film ever made. If it was intended as a put-on, it's one of the great science-fiction satires. The story is simple. An alien colossus transforms Allison Hayes into a giant. She is trapped, escapes, and goes after her adulterous husband. She finds him, kills his mistress (in the local ice-cream parlor), and then destroys both herself and hubby Harry. The effects, acting, script, photography, editing, and directing are so inept as to leave no doubt that they were intentionally so.

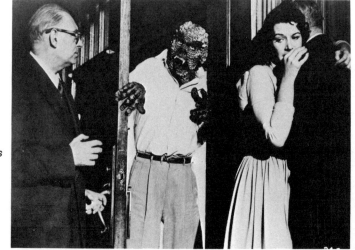

Impressive monster make-up was about the only redeeming factor in The Hideous Sun Demon, *starring Robert Clarke as the monster.*

Moving from the tall to the supersmall, after passing through a strange mist, Grant Williams became 1957's *Incredible Shrinking Man*. The perils he must face—such as gargantuan tarantula and an equally menacing household cat—are many, not the least of which is the man's concern for his future: He cannot stop shrinking. The film ignores much of the profundity found in the original Richard Matheson novel. Williams's musings about his eventually shrinking to atomic size and finding worlds within atoms, shrinking still further and finding even smaller worlds, and so forth, are left to a short, unclear soliloquy at the film's conclusion. Nonetheless, the work is intelligent, frightening, warm, and strong in character development and special effects.

One of the few flawless science fiction–horror films is the 1958 nightmare *The Fly*. Al Hedison—before he became David Hedison and an officer on the *Seaview* in TV's *Voyage to the Bottom of the Sea*—experimenting with a matter transmitter, attempts to transport himself from one room to another. Unbeknownst to Hedison, however, a fly enters the booth; both he and the bug are disintegrated and beamed across the laboratory. When they rematerialize, the scientist has the head and leg of the fly, and the fly owns Hedison's head and arm. The fly itself (with the scientist's head) is eventually devoured by a spider, and Hedison (with the fly's head and succumbing rapidly to its instinct and will) destroys himself by crushing his alien members beneath a giant mechanical press. The script and performances are top notch, and the finest sequence in the film is the one in which Hedison—losing his mind to that of the fly—scrawls on a laboratory blackboard, to his horrified wife, "I love you."

A sequel, *Return of the Fly* (1959), features the scientist's son monkeying around with papa's old equipment. The plot is formula material, and the film loses its slickness to sensationalism. The one effective sequence in *Return of the Fly* has a man and guinea pig placed in the transmitter, their atoms merging en route to produce a rather bizarre hybrid.

The best that can be said about *The Alligator People* (1959) is that it's *different*. It's the story of a scientist who hopes to grow new limbs on unwilling subjects with injections of *l'essence d'alligator* but turns them, instead, into human reptiles.

A similar fate befell *The Hideous Sun Demon* (1959), a scientist who turns into a scale-caked beast when exposed to the light of day. An interesting reverse werewolf theme and wholly convincing makeup elevate this film to a notch above average.

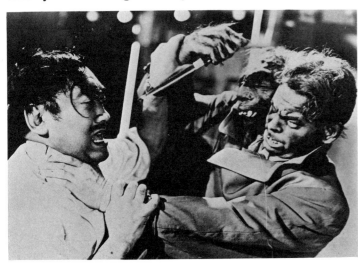

The Manster attacks his creator in this Japanese thriller.

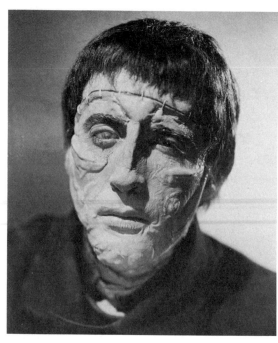

Christopher Lee as the monster in
Curse of Frankenstein.

Another of the better entries in the man-into-monster field is *The Creeping Unknown* (1956), first in a series of three films featuring the British Dr. Quatermass. This work centers around the sole survivor of a three-man spaceflight. As the film progresses, it is discovered that the man is possessed by an alien life form that slowly turns the former astronaut into a giant fungus-like monstrosity that absorbs the life essence from all living things. Trapped in Westminster Abbey, the menace is obliterated.

That same year, convict Lon Chaney was brought back from the dead to avenge his execution in *The Indestructible Man.*

The Manster (1961) was a Japanese import about a mock-Jekyll American correspondent subjected to a formula that personifies his evil self and finally breaks from his body. More provocative was *4-Sided Triangle* (1953), a film about science's effort to form duplicate people using Barbara Payton as a guinea pig. *Creature With the Atom Brain* (1955) was a minor effort in which a scientist revives the dead for evil purposes; the same theme was used more effectively that same year in *The Gamma People* with Communists, rather than an American gangster, the antagonists.

Good, but only barely so, is *Donovan's Brain* (1953), yet another of those interminable brain-in-a-tank pictures. The same idea was better done on several occasions, most notably on TV's *Way Out* and *The Outer Limits.* The film's only plus is the performance of Gene Evans.

Another strong, often compelling performance (by Robert Lansing) is the only redeeming feature of an awful film known as *The 4-D Man* (1959). Scientist Lansing finds a way to make himself able to pass through solid matter. Naturally, he turns to crime. There are one or two effective sequences in the film—such as when Lansing, early in his experiments, puts his hand through a metal block and can't get it out again—but as a whole, the picture is a minor, unconvincing effort. The 4-D Man is never killed, by the way; no doubt the studio hoped for a sequel.

Allison Hayes is not very happy about having seen a giant from space in Attack of the Fifty Foot Woman.

In *The Atomic Kid* (1954), Mickey Rooney is caught eating a peanut-butter sandwich on the test site for an atomic bomb. When the weapon goes off, Rooney turns radioactive. What follows is a lot of espionage and assorted hogwash. Even worse, however, is *The Amazing Transparent Man* (1959), a pitiful—though mercifully short (fifty-six minutes)—rehashing of the invisible-man theme.

After a ten-year vacation, Dr. Frankenstein was hard at work creating new and deadly monsters, and the father of the fifties Frankenstein films was *Curse of Frankenstein* (1957), first of many British Hammer entries in the Frankenstein saga. *Curse of Frankenstein* was essentially a remake of the classic Karloff film (featuring Christopher Lee as the monster), while the 1958 sequel, *Revenge of Frankenstein,* features Michael Gwynn as a new Frankenstein's monster, more twisted psychologically than physically.

Frankenstein's Daughter is an American quickie that features an average plot, average acting, pitiful makeup, and poor casting. The star was Harold Lloyd, Jr., as Dr. Frankenstein. This feeble 1959 effort was complemented by another major disappointment that year, Boris Karloff's first and only appearance as the good doctor Frankenstein in *Frankenstein 1970,* featuring a crew of moviemakers menaced by Frankenstein's latest monster as they shoot a horror film at the scientist's castle.

Bert I. Gordon straddled two extremes of the man-into-monster genre with his films *The Cyclops* (1955) and *Attack of the Puppet People* (1957). The Cyclops was·a flier downed amid radioactive fields who subsequently grew to giant proportions. Of course, the fellow's face was badly mutilated in the crash, and the result was an obvious inspiration for the monster in *War of the Colossal Beast. Attack of the Puppet People* featured people shrunk to doll size by a lonely old scientist. Both films are entertaining, although the special effects—especially in *The Cyclops*—suffer because of budgetary limitations. One must suspect that since Mr. Gordon can do excellent effects work (as in *The Magic Sword*), he let his commercial—rather than artistic—emotions get the best of him.

MAN IN SPACE

Years before Sputnik and Explorer, Hollywood was taking us to the moon and beyond. Of the many flights of fancy in which filmmakers indulged, however, one towers above all others. *Forbidden Planet* (1956) is without peer; it's easily the most awesome science-fiction spectacle ever made. The plot, based loosely and curiously on Shakespeare's *The Tempest,* is complex. A shipload of spacemen land on Altair Four, a planet colonized years before by a handful of earthmen. Of the original party, there is but one survivor. He is Morbius, a linguist. The other colonists were destroyed by some inexplicable planetary force to which only Morbius—and his wife, who died subsequently of natural causes—is immune.

e Lunar Eagle
s reached its
al in
stination Moon.

Herald Square in
New York City is
flooded in
When Worlds Collide.

The film evolves into a life-and-death struggle between the new arrivals, Morbius, and the mysterious planetary force. This force, it is eventually discovered, is Morbius' animalistic Id personified and made real by power drawn from ages-old machinery built by a now-extinct race of beings known as the Krell.

Forbidden Planet was a resounding commercial success. It has startling special effects (nominated for an Oscar, they lost to John P. Fulton's *Ten Commandments* work),[7] a clever and original electronic-music score, fine production values, clever in-studio sets and props . . . and Anne Francis looking properly sexy as Morbius' daughter in futuristic garb.

Walter Pidgeon is excellent as Morbius, maintaining the image of devoted father and

Work progresses on the spaceship that will carry forty humans to safety in When Worlds Collide.

scientist, yet sufficiently menacing to invoke visions of the devil; Leslie Nielsen and Warren Stevens are good, if a bit stiff, as the intrepid leaders of the expedition to Altair Four. And *Forbidden Planet* was the vehicle for the screen debut of Robby the Robot, as classy and quaint a robot as the science-fiction film has seen. Irwin Allen patterned the robot in his television series *Lost in Space* after this extremely popular character.

At times loud and frenzied, literally encircling the viewer with sight, sound, and fury, and at other times subtle and silently unnerving, *Forbidden Planet* is, on every conceivable level, a work of commercial art.

Another fine film, though it became dated, is George Pal's *Destination Moon* (1950). It, along with the cheap but big-box-office *Rocketship XM* (1950), features humanity reaching for the moon. In Pal's story, based on Robert Heinlein's Spaceship Galileo, an independently financed spaceflight gets to the moon and back with the help of some

The Space Ark picks up speed as it rockets down the runway en route to another world. From When Worlds Collide.

Space Ark lands on Zyra from When Worlds Collide.

startling special effects and lavish art direction. The crew of Rocketship XM is diverted from its course by a meteor swarm and lands on Mars.

On the other hand, Joseph Cotten and company do make it *From the Earth to the Moon* (1958), but the film is a stiff and lifeless adaptation of the Jules Verne masterpiece. Equally ineffective is *Project Moon Base* (1953), an anti-Communist effort based on a novel by Robert Heinlein, while *Flight to Mars* was standard fare for 1951 featuring Cameron Mitchell as the commander of a flight that journeys beneath the surface of the red planet.

George Pal returned to space twice within the next few years, first with *Conquest of Space* (1955), an awful film about the first landing on Mars. The film features preparations— aboard a space station orbiting a thousand miles above the earth—for the historic trip. Veterans Philip Yordan, G. W. Yates, and James O'Hanlon were responsible for the screenplay, and upon their conscience must rest such lines as, "Do you realize I've been up here on this tin doughnut for over a year without leave?" and narration in which a somber voice intones "This is a story of tomorrow . . . or the day after tomorrow." Byron

The original ad art, sans copy, for Forbidden Planet.

Leslie Nielsen forces Walter Pidgeon to face his Id Monster as daughter Anne Francis looks on. From Forbidden Planet.

Anne Francis poses with Robby the Robot behind the scenes in Forbidden Planet.

Haskin's direction was made intentionally subservient to the technical aspects of the film, which is unfortunate, since John P. Fulton's special-effects work is below par.

A more professional and satisfying film is Pal's striking adaptation of Philip Wylie's science-fiction classic *When Worlds Collide* (1951). The film won an Oscar for its breathtaking special effects. In the story, a runaway planet is on a collision course with Earth. Financed by a millionaire who wants not to be here when worlds collide, a group of scientists build a space ark that will carry them to a habitable satellite of the stray world. Thanks to this effort, forty earthlings survive.

Less fortunate were those luckless theatergoers who went along for a ride to *The Angry Red Planet* (1959). This movie features some of the worst acting and special effects in history. One must see the ridiculous bat-rat-spider-crab to believe it. Bert I. Gordon undertook an even more absurd excursion to the planet Nova in *King Dinosaur* (1955). Backed by stock footage galore, a group of astronauts fly to a newly discovered planet and, landing on an island, find lizards pretending to be prehistoric monsters. The film has one strong point—a solid musical score by Gene Garf.

The futuristic spaceship from Forbidden Planet *approaches Altair-4.*

Back on Mars, a manned expedition to that planet picks up a most unwelcome stowaway —*It! The Terror from Beyond Space* (1958), a Martian monster that is both brutal and bloody. After wreaking all sorts of havoc on board the spaceship, the monster is escorted —via a sudden vacuum—through a hatchway and into space.

Two movies that deserve to be shot into space are *Catwomen of the Moon* (1953) and *Queen of Outer Space* (1958). Both had low budgets; worse, however, they had no acting, plot, or intelligence. A third disaster, *Missile to the Moon* (1959), at least had some interesting rock creatures, along with a lost race of women and giant spider. In the only impressive sequence of the film, an astronaut—in reality, a gangster who stole the rocketship and, with a friend, made for the moon—is chased unprotected into the sunlight of the moon by these rock men and is burned to a crisp. Other than that, the film is hilarious.

Not so funny is *Abbott and Costello Go to Mars* (1953), wherein the pair ends up on Venus and finds a civilization of beauties. The film is redeemed only by the presence of veteran actor Horace McMahon. Not quite as bad is *Have Rocket Will Travel* (1959), a Three Stooges effort that is not without charm. It features a flame-throwing monster tarantula, a friendly talking unicorn, and duplicate robot stooges on Venus.

Both *X-15* (1961) and *Breaking the Sound Barrier* (1952) are told in semidocumentary form, but only the latter is heir to any real maturity. The story of a millionaire's demonic drive to develop the jet plane, *Breaking the Sound Barrier* is David Lean at his meticulous best. *X-15,* its feet set firmly in fifties format, bogs down in heavy-handed melodrama.

A luckless victim of scientific advances is the *First Man into Space* (1959), who returns to earth—after being exposed to cosmic rays—encased in a mineral crust. *Riders to the Stars* (1954) is an interesting idea gone wrong, the story of an effort to pluck meteors from space to determine what substance protects them from the ravages of extraterrestrial travel. The film falters because of low budget, awful acting, and inept directing. On the other hand, *Spaceways* (1953), which revolves around satellites, spaceships, and an interplanetary murder mystery, hasn't even a good plot. Then there's *War of the Satellites* (1958), simply another alien takeover of a scientific mind.

From the far reaches of space we travel to the bottom of the sea and the incomparable artistry of Walt Disney. Disney was responsible for one of the most startling journeys ever, a trip that takes us *Twenty Thousand Leagues under the Sea* (1954). The film features a stellar cast headed by Kirk Douglas and James Mason, not to mention a marvelous, thoroughly convincing mechanically operated monster squid with whom the submariners do battle. Another Disney-Verne movie, *In Search of the Castaways* (1960), featured Maurice Chevalier and Hayley Mills, but despite the presence of a kidnapping monster bird, it was not up to Disney's earlier effort.

Jules Verne provided the vehicle for another highly successful fantasy–science-fiction film in *Journey to the Center of the Earth* (1959). James Mason stood once again in the fore, this time in charge of an expedition to the earth's core. With him were, among others,

On the surface of the Forbidden
Planet.

Pat Boone and Arlene Dahl. The film features fantastic and colorful sets, lizards convincingly accoutered with fins to resemble prehistoric dimetrodons, and fine acting, not to mention a superb musical score by the great Bernard Herrmann.

Had Mason made the trip three years earlier, he'd have run into John Agar, who had tunneled deep beneath the Asian continent and discovered the lost race of *The Mole People.*

Back in space we find the most maligned film in science-fiction-film history, one that is used, wrongly, as an example of all that is bad in science fiction film making. To be sure, *Fire Maidens of Outer Space* (1956) is absurd, but it is not without appeal. In the story, five men journey to the thirteenth moon of Jupiter and discover what is left of the ancient terrestrial civilization of Atlantis. As Prossus, the ruler of New Atlantis explains it, "Here [Atlantis] is in all its splendor, but there are only a few of us [Prossus and two dozen lovely ladies] left. With your help, gentlemen, New Atlantis will rise stronger than ever; once again New Atlantis shall rule!"

The old man has been keeping the girls prisoner in his Jovian mini-empire, awaiting the day when a rocket from Earth will arrive and the passengers will help repopulate Atlantis, providing Prossus with many subjects. Needless to say, the astronauts get the gals after Prossus is destroyed and a guardian monster is done in, and all ends happily. The Fire Maidens, incidentally, are so called because of a religious ceremony they perform.

Certainly, the film is silly, but it makes no pretense of sophistication. The actors are not good, but they tackle their roles with heft and determination. The film's effort to entertain cannot be maligned. And, if for historical value alone, the movie features a background score of classical music lifted, primarily, from Borodin, ten years before Kubrick. At worst, *Fire Maidens of Outer Space* can be accused of being nothing less than light entertainment.[8]

Two views of incredibly phony monsters from King Dinosaur.

INVADERS FROM SPACE

The greatest of the invaders from space and one of the finest science fiction films of all time is *The Thing from Another World* (1951). The film tells of a flying saucer discovered beneath the Arctic surface. Upon impact, the craft threw its occupant from the ship, and the being immediately froze. A team of American soldiers and scientists removes the creature in a frozen block and takes it to an Arctic outpost where the Thing is kept on ice.

While awaiting further orders, the men inadvertently allow the creature to thaw and the space being escapes. Eventually we learn that the Thing is a vegetable in humanoid form and is most likely the advance scout for an invasion of bloodthirsty creatures from space. The Thing is finally burned to death by electricity, but not before causing several heinous deaths and maimings.

The monster is kept in shadow throughout the film; never once do we get a good look at it. This technique, somewhat similar to the way James Whale kept Karloff's *Frankenstein* (1931) in shadow for a good portion of that film, creates a presence of lurking horror in which our imagination supplies all the details. One sequence in particular, when the invader bursts into a room in which the soldiers are waiting in ambush, is filmed, at first, by what little light there is in the darkened room. Illumination comes only when the monster throws open the door and is doused with kerosene and set ablaze. The action of the scene is rapid, artistic effects notwithstanding. The takes were quick because a man was actually set afire for realism. Before the monster leaps through a window and runs into the Arctic night, he overturns men and furniture in a frenetic, wholly frightening battle.

The players in *The Thing* are not fictional characters of the year 2000, but men of today. Their actions and reactions are credible, and the interplay between the earthmen and the space being, the dialogue, and the crisp, taut directing elevate *The Thing* to classic proportions.

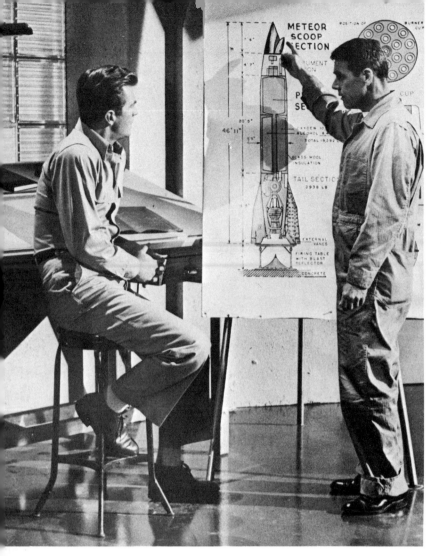

NASA take note: Back in 1954, it took but two men to design a workable spaceship. Herbert Marshall and William Lundigan discuss the plans for a spaceship that will snare meteors in order to discover what material coats and protects them from the rigors of interstellar travel. From Riders to the Stars.

A look at the ship that will carry Howard Duff and Eva Bartok into earth orbit in Spaceways.

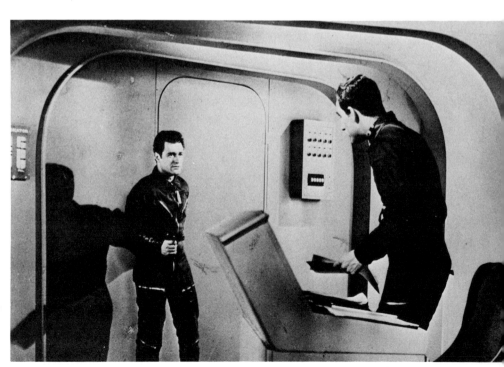

Confrontation between hero and villain in War of the Satellites, a film that played on a double bill with Attack of the Fifty Foot Woman.

The men of the Nautilus *battle the giant squid in Walt Disney's* Twenty Thousand Leagues Under the Sea.

Another classic, epic in scope and intellect, is *This Island Earth* (1955). It has everything —fine actors, a mature, sturdy script, a realistic and terrifying monster, flying saucers, and flawless, utterly astounding special effects. There are few subplots in this story of the kidnapping of two American scientists to the planet Metaluna, a world at war with another planet, and although the scientists and their alien hosts do not leave Earth until midway through the film, the production is never dull or condescending. This is a thoroughly professional work. The flaming finale alone is worth the price of admission . . . if you are lucky enough to find it playing somewhere.[9]

A third masterpiece is the 1956 film *Invasion of the Body Snatchers.* Dropping hints along the way that "something is very wrong in this town," the picture moves from a mood of subtle horror to one of out-and-out panic. In the story, seed pods from outer space form duplicates of human bodies, perfect in every detail, and take over their human counterparts as the victims sleep.

Physician Kevin McCarthy discovers what's going on and, after a series of near captures and flights into terror, manages to flee the contaminated town to warn the outside world. The film is not technically innovative, but it is impressive in the way it creates an aura of stark reality about the goings-on. All the characters—as in *The Thing*—are believable; they are people who might be anyone's next-door neighbors. And therein lies the film's

Kirk Douglas carries an unconscious seaman below in
Twenty Thousand Leagues Under the Sea.

fright potential. If one accepts the basic premise of extraterrestrial seed pods—and why not; who knows what sort of alien debris is floating through space?—then the rest of the action flows naturally and fluidly. The film is low key and unpretentious and one of the most credible science-fiction films this side of *The Andromeda Strain* (1971).

Robert Wise's *The Day the Earth Stood Still* (1951) is a brilliant film about a visit from space by Klaatu (Michael Rennie) and a ten-foot-tall robot named Gort. Klaatu makes the voyage to warn Earth that continued misuse of space and atomic weaponry will result in our total obliteration. Mincing few words and wasting little time, he demonstrates his power on a minor scale by shutting down all man's electrical energy for a half hour.

Klaatu is subsequently shot to death, but his corpse is recovered by a vengeful Gort, and he is revived within the security of his saucer. Before returning to space, he delivers the finest soliloquy in science-fiction-film history.

Soon one of your nations will apply atomic power to rockets. Up to now we have not cared how you solved your petty squabbles. But if you threaten to extend your violence, this Earth of yours will be reduced to a burned-out cinder. Your choice is simple. Join us and live in peace. Or pursue your present course and face obliteration. The decision rests with you.

A pitiful attempt to remake *The Day the Earth Stood Still* came in 1959 and went by the name of *Cosmic Man.* The film features the usually distinguished John Carradine lurking menacingly in trench coat and dark glasses.

Equally absurd—but with a little something for the eye, if not the mind—is the 1958 atrocity *The Astounding She-Monster.* In this one a sexy female invader in sequins and a skin-tight uniform wreaks havoc among the inhabitants of a ski lodge. And she glows!

The classic undersea burial sequence from Twenty Thousand Leagues Under the Sea.

James Mason in Twenty Thousand Leagues Under the Sea.

A view from the bridge of the Nautilus. From Twenty Thousand Leagues Under the Sea.

The Space Children (1958) is a film wherein (another!) giant brain from space takes over the children of scientists, using the kids to stop their parents' work on atomic warheads. Director Jack Arnold has done better.

A magnificent sequence in which Tor Johnson rises from the grave is the only redeeming element of *Plan Nine from Outer Space,* a 1959 disaster that was unfortunately the last screen appearance of the great Bela Lugosi. For the record, the film features aliens that visit the earth in search of zombies.

Not surprisingly, the only zombies visible in *Teenagers from Outer Space* (1959) were people who went to see the film. A group of space teens comes to take over Earth; their plans go awry when one of them falls in love with an Earth girl and betrays his comrades. The picture sports a giant crab monster—named the Gargon—or so we're told. All that's ever shown is the creature's shadow.

Brain from Planet Arous (1957) is an often effective thriller of a flying ocular brain from space that takes over John Agar's body in hopes of conquering the universe. It is thwarted by a "good" brain from Arous. *The Brain Eaters* (1958) do their thing via small puncture wounds in their victims' necks, and no brains at all are evident in *Phantom from Space* (1953), the story of an invisible visitor from the stars.

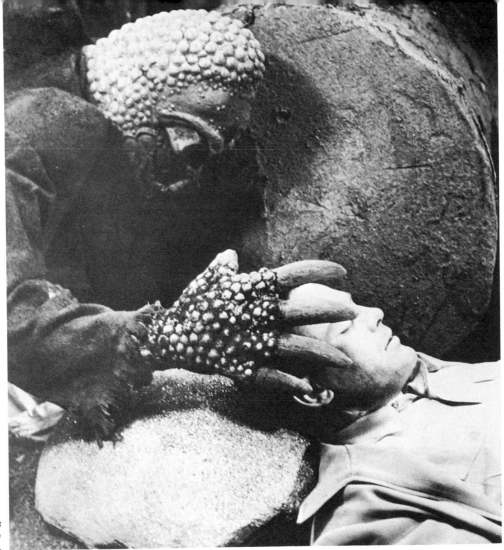

Pat Boone in one of the incredible sets for Journey to the Center of the Earth.

John Agar is about to have his head crushed by one of the Mole People.

The charming Mole People, in the film of the same name.

*Exeter's spaceship comes in for a
landing on Metaluna in* This
Island Earth.

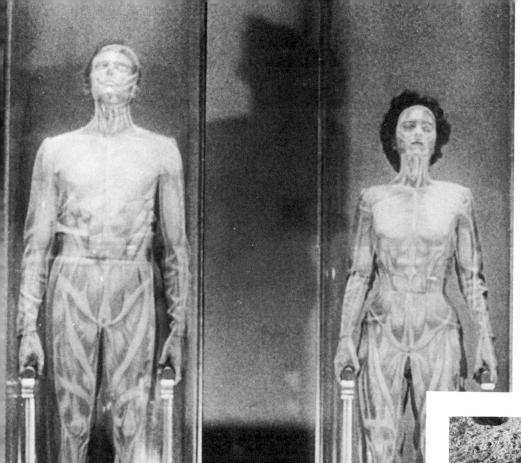

Rex Reason and Faith Domergue undergo decompression as their spaceship slows from speeds faster than that of light. From This Island Earth.

A view of the subterranean city of the planet Metaluna. From This Island Earth.

Exeter (Jeff Morrow, left) shows Rex Reason and Faith Domergue the bridge of his starship. From This Island Earth.

Jeff Morrow, Rex Reason, and Faith Domergue run from one building to another beneath the surface of the besieged Metaluna. From This Island Earth.

Conversely, *The Man from Planet X* (1951) overcomes a minuscule budget to provide a little more than an hour's worth of atmosphere and mild entertainment. Intent on invading earth, Planet X sends a pasty-looking entity to a small Scottish town with the mission of hypnotizing the inhabitants for use in the invasion. His mission and his life are cut short by army bazookas. Then we are visited by *Killers from Space* (1953), one of the cheapest, most absurd films ever made. This one has alien beings breeding giant insects and lizards with which they hope to conquer the world. Not even a stoic Peter Graves can save the film from obvious makeup and even worse special effects.

I Married a Monster from Outer Space (1958) is an interesting film in which Gloria Talbott discovers that the man she thinks is her husband is really an alien advance scout for an invasion. Despite the silly title, the film is intriguing and well done. Tom Tryon, who went on the play Walt Disney's *Moon Pilot* (1960) and write the bestselling novel *The Other*, portrays the alien visitor.

A TV set from space lands in the house of Hans Conried in Arch Oboler's unsubtle but clever film fantasy *The Twonky* (1953). After subjugating the minds of several Earthlings, the TV set is hurled from a cliff by Conried. But unknown to the star, baby TV sets crawl from the murdered parent.

Not from space, but from three thousand years hence, comes *The Terror from the Year 5,000* (1958), a pathetically mutated female who visits the twentieth century via an accident of science.

Soldiers arrive at the crash-site of a flying saucer. Using thermal bombs, they free a creature frozen beneath the surface of the ice. From The Thing.

Two completely different ad art renderings for The Thing.

The block of ice containing an eight-foot-tall Thing arrives at an Arctic military outpost.

The Thing approaches, and soldiers prepare to electrocute the humanoid vegetable.

Kenneth Tobey is none too happy about the fact that Robert Cornethwaite (to his right) has been feeding tiny seed pods from space the base's store of blood plasma. From The Thing.

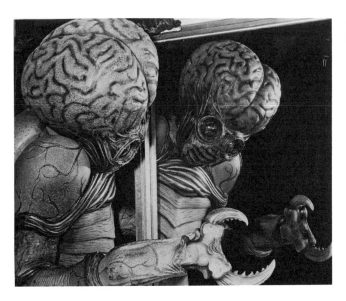

The bug-like Metaluna Mutant from This Island Earth.

An unfortunate scientist is about to have his life cut short by the alien astronaut in The Creeping Unknown.

The 27th Day (1957) is McCarthy-era propaganda about a being from space who gives capsules to a select group of Earthlings. These capsules, if opened, will ostensibly destroy all life on Earth. The Communists get hold of a capsule and are about to open it, when their American counterpart (Gene Barry) figures out how to open his capsule and direct its power to a specific latitude and longitude, destroying the Communists first. At a meeting of the United Nations after the destruction of the Soviet Union, the aliens are invited to settle on Earth and live with us in harmony. The film is well acted and has a strong script; unfortunately, from today's perspective, it is an embarrassing work.

The Monolith Monsters (1957) is a superb and engrossing film about crystals from space that, in addition to turning people to stone, grow to monstrous heights when exposed to water. The special effects, especially the sound effects, are excellent.

Enemy from Space (1957) involves will-enslaving invaders in the second of the British Professor Quatermass films, and the *Invaders from Mars* (1953) are a group of bug-eyed beings controlled by a small tentacled creature in a glass dome. Anyone who happens near their buried saucer is sucked through the sand and has a device imbedded in his brain that puts the Martians in control of his will. The saucer is finally invaded by soldiers and blown to smithereens.

Flame Barrier (1958) is the device through which an alien, after riding to earth aboard a satellite, protects itself from the prying eyes of Arthur Franz. The film, set in an exotic and well-appointed Mexican jungle, tries hard but doesn't quite make it. Far more successful is the 1953 adaptation of Ray Bradbury's *It Came from Outer Space*. Filmed in 3-D, it's the story of creatures that crash-land on Earth and don't really want to stay. With neither the manpower nor the materials to effect repairs, the aliens take over the minds and bodies of Earthlings, fix their disabled craft, and leave. The film is well made, the acting is solid, and the result is the finest Bradbury-to-film effort to date.

Not of This Earth (1957), on the other hand, is one of those science-fiction films in which the invader dons dark glasses and a trench-coat, has a visicommunicator through which

Brian Donlevy discusses the
arrival of the Enemy From Space
with an assistant.

Kevin McCarthy spies a monster
seed pod in his cellar. From The
Invasion of the Body Snatchers.

he confers with superiors, and kills people by stuffing them into incinerators as well as doing them in with flying batlike emissaries. Yet as bad as the film is, it's better by leaps and bounds than *War of the Satellites* (1957), a sickly motion picture in which a scientist killed in a crash is taken over by aliens seeking to sabotage a satellite project. It's the worst space film until 1963's *Battle of the Worlds*.

John Carradine strikes again as one of the corpses occupied by the *Invisible Invaders* (1959), alien entities finally done in by John Agar and blasts of high-frequency sound. *Invasion of the Saucer Men* (1957) is another of those teenagers-versus-aliens films; however, there is something to be said for this effort. It is what amounts to a satire wherein diminutive creatures from space inject alcohol into bloodstreams of their victims, making them drunk; naturally, when the unfortunates run to the police, their story of alien invaders is not believed. The creatures are eliminated when teenagers unite and disintegrate them with the high-intensity beams from their auto headlights.

X—The Unknown (1957) was a mysterious invader from the Earth's core. The film features Anthony Newley, who might well have asked himself "What Kind of Fool Am I?" for getting stuck in this British disappointment. But in a way, the title suggests an impasse against which filmmakers had fallen: What do we do *next* for an invader from space? A noted photographer once said of his art, "If you can't do it right, do it in color. If it still doesn't work, do it *big*." That's exactly what was done.

Klaatu comes forth to make an offering of peace. From The Day the Earth Stood Still.

Mistaking Klaatu's gift for a weapon, soldiers fell Klaatu with a round of fire. From The Day the Earth Stood Still.

Michael Rennie

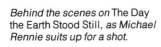

Behind the scenes on The Day the Earth Stood Still, as Michael Rennie suits up for a shot.

Klaatu and Gort emerge from their spacecraft. From The Day the Earth Stood Still.

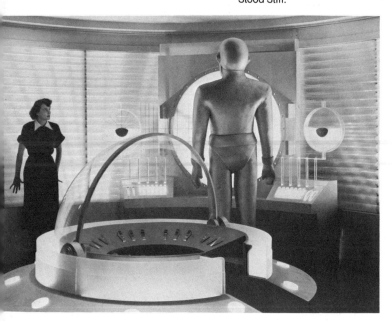

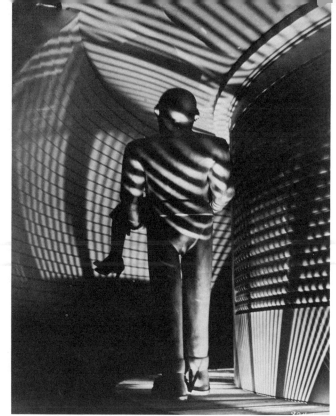

Gort kidnaps a stunned Patricia Neal. From The Day the Earth Stood Still.

KING-SIZE VISITORS FROM SPACE

A popular variation of the atomic-bomb-born monster on the loose was the giant monster from space on the loose. The uncontested king of this genre is Ray Harryhausen's masterful *Twenty Million Miles to Earth* (1957). This picture has an adequate script, above-average acting, and characters that are blatantly used as pawns to further the action. It has also the finest alien monster and special effects ever created for a film of this type. An egg, bearing the creature known as Ymir, is brought back from Venus by the first manned expedition to that planet. Encased in the small, jellylike egg, the beast hatches and begins to grow. Within days, it reaches epic proportions and, after running rampant through the ruins of Rome, is felled from atop the Colosseum.

Of all Mr. Harryhausen's monsters, the Ymir has the most vivid and enthralling personality. He is a vicious, frightening creature: Unlike *King Kong*—the 1933 grandfather of all the animated monsters who, despite his simian nature, possessed sensitivity and the capacity for tenderness—Ymir is wholly bestial.

In his efforts to survive the hostilities of Earth, Ymir dispatches men and buildings with understandable lack of concern. Indeed, not content with having his monster further destroy the ruins of Rome, Harryhausen pits his Venusian against an elephant in what has to be the strangest, most one-sided battle in film history.[10] Setting the film in Rome gives it travelogue appeal, and seeing a creature from outer space traipsing about the ancient ruins is an anachronistic pleasure.

Of particular interest in this, the first of Harryhausen's Dynamation[11] films, is the opening sequence, in which the rocket from Venus is shown returning to Earth, pushing through the skies and into the Mediterranean with a bulk and thrust that hardly betray the fact that it is

From left to right, Bruce Bennett, Paul Langton, Harry Fleer, and Lyn Osborne eye the spaceship of The Cosmic Man.

A peek at the giant brain, master of The Space Children.

One of the Teenagers from Outer Space arrives on earth.

Arnold Moss is a being from outer space in The 27th Day.

Tom Tryon as the featured creature in I Married a Monster From Outer Space.

The Man from Planet X performs an experiment.

a miniature model. Putting forth the finest animated effort of his career, Harryhausen elevates a second-rate thriller to classic proportions.

Any film that contains the line "You keep your shirts on and I'll go put my pants on" can't be all bad. And *The Giant Claw* (1957) is *not* all bad. It has some great stock footage from *Earth vs. the Flying Saucers* (1956), as well as a passable shot of the monster's claw reaching heavenward as the creature sinks slowly beneath the surface of the sea after being shot from the sky. But that's it. The rest of the film is a tragedy. The Giant Claw is actually a monstrous bird from space that visits Earth to lay an egg. Unfortunately, that is what the producers of this turkey did even before the aviary alien arrived.

Better by far is England's *The Crawling Eye* (1958). Weak on special effects, the film is strong on atmosphere, mood, suspense, acting, and script. It's the story of space monsters hiding in a cloud—which they made for cover—that clings to the side of a mountain in the Alps. After killing several mountain climbers, the monsters move with their cloud into Trollenberg, a small, isolated town at the foot of the peak where the tension becomes real and severe, a flawlessly constructed nightmare. And here is as fine a collection of actors as one is likely to find in a science-fiction film in the fifties. Janet Munro and Forrest Tucker are superb. Tucker was seen again combatting *The Cosmic Monsters* (1958), but for sheer fright value and all-around class, it can't hold a candle to *The Crawling Eye.*

From one giant orb we move to *The Beast With a Million Eyes* (1955), a mildly diverting vehicle wherein a space monster takes over the bodies of people and farm animals. Taking refuge in the body of a desert rodent, the creature is devoured by an eagle.

From Venus came the most absurd-looking monster ever, created by Paul Blaisdell, who should have known better, in *It Conquered the World* (1956). A better film is *Atomic Submarine* (1959), in which a specially constructed sea vehicle goes in search of an extraterrestrial force that has buried itself beneath the North Pole. Arthur Franz is the man in charge who finally comes face to eye with an enormous living spaceship and its self-duplicating cyclopean inhabitant.

After they've been possessed by an alien intelligence, the parents of Jimmy Hunt come looking for the boy. From Invaders From Mars.

Luckily, Helena Carter will not turn Jimmy Hunt over to Arthur Franz and Hillary Brooke in Invaders From Mars.

103

An astounding, extremely rare special effects scene from The Monolith Monsters.

Richard Carlson comes face to eye with "it" in It Came From Outer Space.

The Blob (1958), starring a youthful Steve McQueen, could have been better. The monster of this film is a gelatinous mass from space that devours people left and right before being frozen and dropped in the Arctic. The acting is tepid, but the effects and photography aren't bad; indeed, the sequence wherein the Blob comes from behind a movie screen is very impressive. Better, though, is the 1972 sequel *Son of Blob*. It, at least, is *intentionally* funny.

ROBOTS, FLYING SAUCERS, AND MACHINES AMOK

H. G. Wells has seen better times than 1953 and George Pal's *War of the Worlds*. Unfortunately, all concerned with the production saw fit to transpose the story from nineteenth-century England to twentieth-century Los Angeles. The change in time and locale destroys much of the inherent flavor of the original novel. Yet the movie survives the update, the stilted, childish dialogue, and Gene Barry's inane acting, primarily on the force of its superb special effects. The Martian war machines, death rays, and scenes of destruction are as gripping and realistic as anything ever created in science-fiction special effects.

A far more successful effort in every way is the 1956 UFO epic *Earth vs. the Flying Saucers*. A fleet of saucers peopled by humanoids in metallic casings comes to Earth to ask permission to relocate from their dying planet. While Earth's powers-that-be stall for time, a group of scientists led by Hugh Marlowe seeks to create a weapon with which to repulse the "peaceable" invaders and their persuasive disintegration ray.

The weapon, which upsets the saucers' equilibrium, causing them to crash, is finished just as the saucermen decide to take Earth by force rather than be civil about it. The climactic battle royal takes place in Washington, D.C., and, thanks to Ray Harryhausen and his animated saucers, the Washington Monument, the Capitol Building, and other historic landmarks tumble before the invaders are defeated and Marlowe wins a Nobel Prize.

Another superior mechanized monster from space, *Kronos* (1957), is nothing more than a robot hundreds of feet tall come to Earth via flying saucer to collect and store all our electric and atomic power. Before this stored power is finally turned against the metallic invader, Kronos destroys cities, power plants, and jet planes and even absorbs the explosive fury of an atom bomb with agility and great aplomb. The special effects are convincing, and Kronos's first appearance—standing stationary on the beach of a small Mexican village—is unique and enticing.

Equally fine are the opening minutes of Japan's 1958 saga *The Mysterians,* in which a giant robot from space—one of the most interesting ever created for a science-fiction film —levels several Japanese cities before being blown to smithereens while crossing a bridge. Unfortunately, the film then degenerates into a typical aliens-looking-for-Earth-women-with-whom-to-intermarry formula potboiler.

Magnetic Monster (1954) served as the pilot for a TV series known as *The Office of Scientific Investigation.* OSI is the organization for which Richard Carlson works in the film. He is called upon to investigate a meteor that falls to Earth and drains the energy from everything that lives. At the film's conclusion the meteor is allowed to OD in an underwater complex, and the resultant explosion is big, loud, and impressive. The screenplay was written by noted science-fiction author Curt Siodmak, the man responsible for *Donovan's Brain.*

Another well-done film is *Gog* (1954), in which international—or intergalactic; we are never told which—espionage in the form of rays from a high-flying aircraft is responsible for death and destruction in an underground lab whose occupants are working on the development of a space station. The internal action focuses on two robots, Gog and Magog, built to perform menial tasks about the complex. Under the influence of the foreign beam, the machines turn on their masters and are destroyed along with the stratospheric intruder.

Then there's *Robot Monster* (1953), a gorilla wearing a space helmet that arrives on Earth to the accompaniment of an Elmer Bernstein score (in his pre–*Magnificent Seven* days), as well as reams of stock footage from, primarily, the 1940 film *One Million B.C.*

A man's brain in the body of a twelve-foot-tall robot—one of the more nightmarish screen robots—is the substance of *Colossus of New York* (1958), and the star of *Tobor the Great* (1954) is a robot built to withstand the stress of space travel. After varied and unnecessary plot twists in which foreign agents plot to turn the robot against us, Tobor finally takes off. The film, however, does not.

The Invisible Boy (1957) is a young lad kidnapped by *Forbidden Planet*'s Robby the Robot in his second screen appearance; the perils and possibilities of a machine (computer or robot) going berserk are interestingly—if in wholly juvenile fashion—outlined by this barely adequate production.

Of more solid quality is Roger Corman's 1954 film *Target Earth!* wherein Richard Denning

Paul Birch snares a pretty victim to satisfy his unearthly desires. From Not of This Earth.

Claude Rains as he appears in one of his last films, Battle of the Worlds.

wakes up to find his town deserted. As the film unfolds, Denning finds other people who were not evacuated when the city was invaded by robots from space. This film, like other Corman works, is much better than it might have been in the hands of a less capable director. Then there was *UFO* (1956), the epitome of the flying-saucer film, being a documentary narrated by saucer sage Tom Powers. It is an interesting film, but hardly convincing. *Earth vs. the Flying Saucers* makes more sense.

MAN, HIS FOLLIES, AND THE END OF THE WORLD

One of the more satisfying entries in the world-has-been-destroyed genre is the 1955 film *World Without End.* A group of astronauts is flung into the year 2508, to discover that three hundred years before, the world had been ravaged and all but annihilated by an atomic war. As the plot thickens, the time travelers discover a race of human beings living underground in comfortable if cramped quarters, facing extinction from a number of sources, while outside dwell hideous mutants and their human slaves.

The new arrivals show the subterranean people how to construct bazookas, and after a few encounters ending in hand-to-hand combat between the astronaut commander and the mutant leader, the mutants are bested and their slaves are freed. The underground race moves from their catacombs to the surface world, and society idyllically begins anew. Despite awful special effects, an obligatory giant spider, and abysmal production values, this film is an intelligent effort with sensible dialogue, a well-paced script, solid acting, and excellent mutant makeup.

The World, the Flesh and the Devil is a film with Harry Belafonte, Inger Stevens, and Mel Ferrer as the three survivors of an atomic war. The 1959 film misses its mark by miles, but does expound—sometimes well, though more often not—moral and racial philosophies in a fashion that elevates it to a tolerable level. It's not nearly as effective, however, as Arch

106

A force from the earth's core makes its presence known in X— the Unknown.

Oboler's frightening and classic film *Five* (1951), the story of the last people left alive after nuclear combat. Tensions grow naturally and are handled in realistic, mature fashion; when a foreign autocrat confronts and kills a black doorman living with a New York City tour guide and his woman, the situation is presented in blunt, all too horrifyingly real terms. The film uses montage, music, and sound effects to great advantage, and the images of a dead Earth are stark and effective. The climactic visit to a once-great metropolis littered with skeletons and debris is credible and well-executed, and it has great impact.

Less arty than *Five* is Stanley Kramer's 1959 *On the Beach*. Based on the novel by Nevil Shute, this is a big-budget, name-star film that, despite some striking individual sequences and performances, doesn't quite stay together as a potent whole. It's the story of post-atomic-war Australia. The rest of the world has blown itself to oblivion while those Down Under await the arrival of the fatally radioactive cloud . . . and death. The end—literally—leaves us an earth devoid of life. But getting to that point in the film is laborious, for the director, despite the best of intentions, too often bogs down in talk and philosophy, neither of which is as fine or eloquent as the photography, which says it all much better.

Two films dealing with national and international doings are *Red Planet Mars* (1952) and *1984* (1955). *1984* is a great disappointment, a lackluster adaptation of the brilliant and frightening George Orwell novel of Big Brother and a totalitarian future. The film tries hard to capture the flavor of the novel, but only scenes of the "breaking" of star Edmund O'Brien through his fear of rats are in any way gripping or true to the novel. The rest of the picture is irrelevant and melodramatic. Much less pretentious, and infinitely finer, is *Red Planet Mars,* an underrated drama in which American scientist Peter Graves makes contact with God, who, it is discovered, lives on Mars. The film eventually gets mixed up in espionage and international intrigue, but the premise is intriguing, and, for the most part it is handled with tact and common sense.

More views of Armageddon than our skilled world can possibly put into quantitative action were unleashed during the fifties. *Captive Women* (1952) tells of mutants versus "Norms" in New York in the year 3,000; seven people and a mediocre Paul Blaisdell mutant-monster survive *The Day the World Ended* (1955). A year before he would become one of John Sturges' *Magnificent Seven*, Robert Vaughn starred as the *Teenage Caveman* (1959); this effort had prehistoric man on Earth years after an atomic war. The audience is not supposed to know that this is man's future and not his past, but by the time Vaughn crosses the "forbidden river" and stumbles upon this "secret," no one cares any more.

Day the Sky Exploded (1957) is an Italian work about a missile that explodes in space and showers debris and panic upon Earth, while *The Night the World Exploded* (1957) follows the day on which a strange element is released from the Earth by atomic detonations. The element explodes on contact with the air and must therefore be "drowned" at the picture's conclusion.

The first manned spaceship to visit the planet Venus returns in Twenty Million Miles to Earth, *only to crash in the Mediterranean Sea off the coast of Sicily.*

A fishing boat makes for the ruins of a great rocket in Twenty Million Miles to Earth.

The rampant Ymir makes a shambles of the already ruined landmarks of Rome. From Twenty Million Miles to Earth.

Ymir, the creature brought back from Venus, escapes from the fallen rocket and hides in a barn. This shot details his capture. From Twenty Million Miles to Earth.

109

Breaking into a zoo, Ymir does battle with an elephant. The elephant, incidentally, is a two-feet-tall stop-motion model, and not a real animal. *From* Twenty Million Miles to Earth.

The drugged Ymir is studied by scientists in Rome. An electrical short circuit awakens the mighty Ymir, who breaks from his bonds and escapes into Rome. *From* Twenty Million Miles to Earth.

Bazooka fire destroys both the top of the Colosseum and the alien Ymir. *From* Twenty Million Miles to Earth.

The amazing war-machines from George Pal's War of the Worlds.

The only shot in existence of the Martians from War of the Worlds.

Commercial airline pilots are the first to see visitors from another world. From Earth vs. the Flying Saucers.

The saucers land, and from within come the humanoid aliens, frail creatures encased in metal. From Earth vs. the Flying Saucers, this shot depicts the aftermath of the destruction of earth's Project Skyhook.

Publicity stills of alien spacecraft menacing Joan Taylor and Hugh Marlowe. From Earth vs. the Flying Saucers.

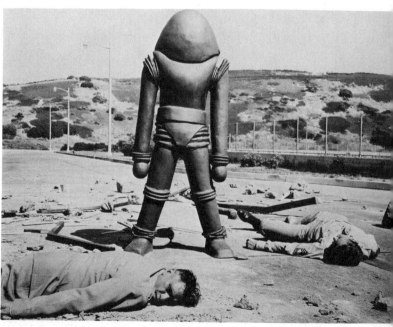

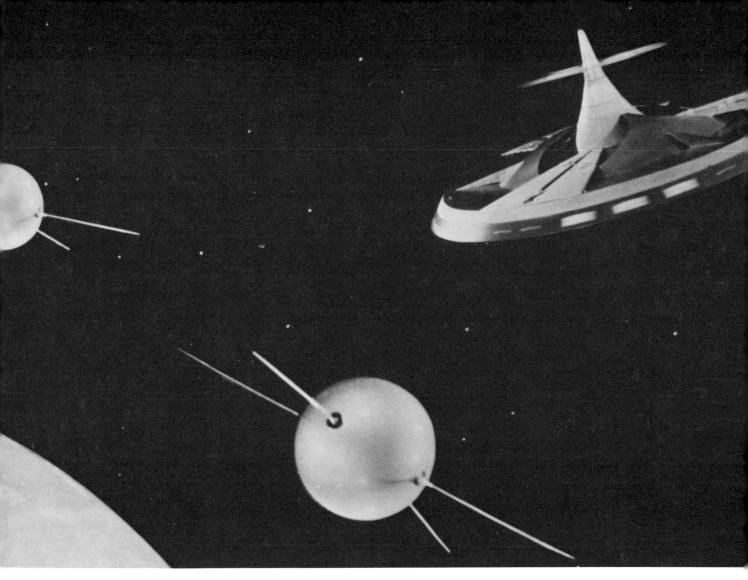

High above the earth orbit the
spaceships of The Mysterians.
The aliens have come to kidnap
and marry earth women.

The Mysterians' *enormous robot
paves the way for their invasion.
Their plans run into a snag when
the monster is blown to pieces as
he crosses a booby-trapped
bridge.*

A31

The robot with the man's brain:
The Colossus of New York.

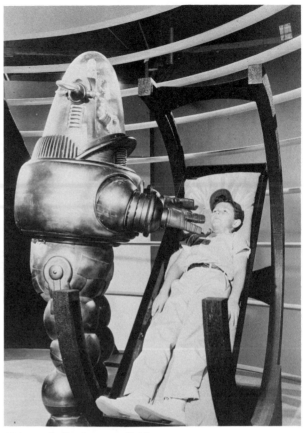

*Millions of miles in space, Robby
the Robot, in his second screen
appearance, prepares to torture
Richard Eyer (who lived, and
went on to play the genie in
Seventh Voyage of Sinbad). From
The Invisible Boy.*

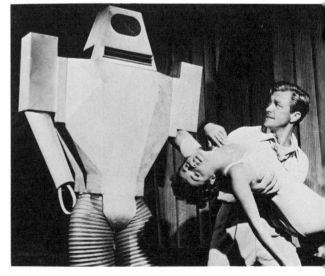

*Richard Denning saves a woman
from the clutches of an outer
space invader-robot in* Target
Earth.

*Military experts analyze
photographs of flying saucers in
the documentary film, UFO.*

The unkempt skyline of New York
City as it appears in Captive
Women.

Lori Nelson and a mutant monster
take in the latest copy of
Imagination. A publicity still from
The Day the World Ended.

A less staid view of the mutant
monster from The Day the World
Ended.

Harry Belafonte realizes that the
end of the world has come, and
he missed it! From World, the
Flesh, and the Devil.

The Sixties

Original ad art for 2001: A Space Odyssey.

The startling sequence wherein, without a single cut, a stewardess on board the Pan-Am clipper walks on the walls! From 2001: A Space Odyssey.

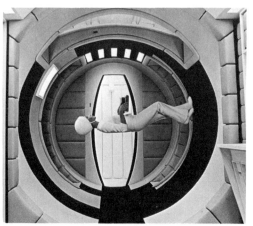

The sixties were a time of great upheaval in all walks of life. Civil rights, Vietnam, the exploration of space, the phenomenal growth of television, violence, and unrest on college campuses were prominent components of this decade. Movies, television, and even comic books emphasized "telling it like it is." And although this more often than not meant "telling it as we see it," science fiction was not averse to accepting social responsibility and fostering political commentary.

The most popular science-fiction film of all time came to us in 1968, courtesy of Stanley Kubrick. His epic film *2001: A Space Odyssey* revolutionized filmmaking. Other meticulously crafted science-fiction films, such as the brilliant *Planet of the Apes* (1968),

116

George Pal's *Time Machine* (1960), and Richard Fleisher's post-*Barabbas* (featuring his and Rome's simultaneous decline) and highly overrated *Fantastic Voyage* (1965), made science fiction popular outside the habitual circle of devotees.

In general, the audience of the sixties was more demanding. On a purely commercial note, they would now be paying three dollars or more to visit a theater that in the fifties, they had entered for ninety cents. Also, humanity had begun its conquest of space, and tolerance for the fantastic, as opposed to that which was of stoic realism, became severely unbalanced in favor of the realistic. Rampant imagination, such as was to be found in *Forbidden Planet* and *This Island Earth,* was replaced by the existential (*Fahrenheit 451*), New Wave (*Alphaville*), and allegorical (*Planet of the Apes*), not to mention the patently ridiculous (*The Green Slime*). Here and there sprouted some of the old formula stuff for the kiddies and the comic-book set—films such as *Beyond the Time Barrier* and *King Kong vs. Godzilla*—but box-office considerations were now intimately merged with intricately crafted special effects, cerebral stimulation, and the "profound."

Therefore, we will begin our look at the science-fiction film of the sixties with that branch most radically influenced by humanity's change in orientation—Man in Space.

 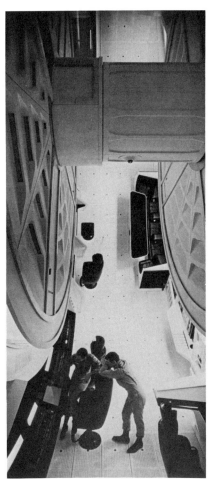 

Aboard the Discovery, *astronauts Keir Dullea and Gary Lockwood prepare to go EVA. From* 2001: A Space Odyssey.

The bridge of the Discovery *in* 2001: A Space Odyssey.

Keir Dullea is reflected in the all-seeing eye of the Discovery's *computer HAL. From* 2001: A Space Odyssey.

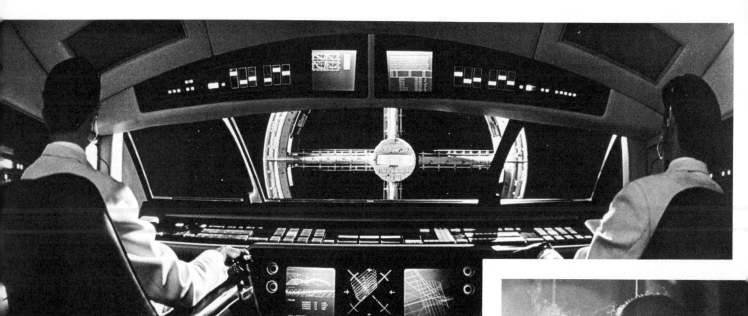

The space clipper glides into its
berth on board the lunar space
station.

Stanley Kubrick directs Gary
Lockwood in a scene from 2001:
A Space Odyssey.

One of the many aircraft that
populate the world of 2001.

MAN IN SPACE

2001: A Space Odyssey (1968) is one of the most original films ever made. From the standpoint of traditional drama, cinema, and structured storytelling, it misses its mark on occasion. It's confusing in spots, unbalanced in emphasizing the strictly pedestrian aspects of plot and characterization, and inexpert in many of its technical aspects. Yet what *The Cabinet of Dr. Caligari* was to the teens, *Potemkin* to the twenties, *Alexander Nevsky* to the thirties, *Citizen Kane* and *Fantasia* to the forties, and Disney's *Sleeping Beauty* to the fifties, *2001: A Space Odyssey* was to the sixties. These films do not

The space station in moon orbit.

A closeup of the unit that HAL erroneously predicts will go 100% failure. From 2001: A Space Odyssey.

Astronaut Lockwood prepares to venture into space to check out HAL's prediction.

HAL is in error, and Lockwood finds nothing wrong with the mechanism. . .

. . . but HAL sees this a perfect
opportunity to kill Lockwood with
a space pod.

After the murder, Dullea gets into
another pod in an effort to retrieve
Lockwood's body. From 2001: A
Space Odyssey.

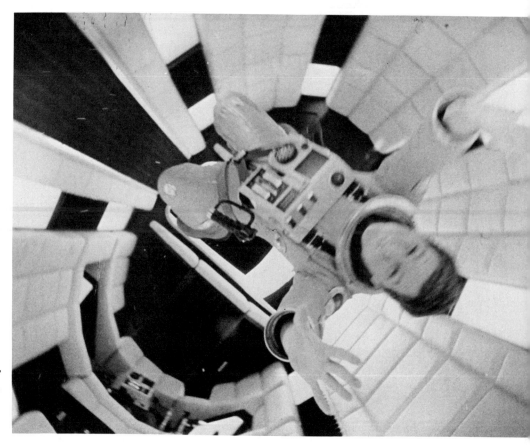

This he does, but HAL will not let him return to the Discovery. Thus, without his helmet, Dullea must reenter the hard way, by blasting his way into the ship. From *2001: A Space Odyssey*.

personify their eras; rather, they exemplify the philosophy—despite comments to the contrary by such film dignitaries as Marlon Brando[12]—that film *can* be an intense, involving art form.

Once the territory of select underground filmmakers—such as Dali and his remarkable *Un Chien Andalou,* a beautifully absurd fantasy—"absolute" film has now become mainstream. In our own decade, this sort of cinema is personified by Bertolucci's *Last Tango in Paris* and Peter Medak's *The Ruling Class.*[13] But *2001: A Space Odyssey,* beyond being a philosophical enigma, is a magnificently tantalizing film. It assaults the mind, eye, and ear with all manner of awesome and stimulating images and suggestions; in showing rather than telling, *2001: A Space Odyssey* has immersed itself in the film medium as have but few pictures before it. Kubrick and Clarke, creators of the concept and screenplay, have been reticent to discuss the film's "meaning," doubtless feeling that to limit it to any one interpretation is to emasculate it as art.

In the story, an alien life form plants "alarm clocks"—represented by large monolithic slabs—in locations throughout the solar system. The first slab, discovered on Earth, endows a prehistoric man-ape with the ability to conceive of using an animal bone as a weapon. When discovered by lunar colonists, the second slab sends a loud shriek toward Jupiter from Earth's moon. The third monolith ensnares, in a space-time vortex, an astronaut who, tracing the second signal, finds himself in orbit around Jupiter with the third slab. The fourth "alarm clock" appears before this astronaut on the weird, wholly distorted (by earthly standards) "world" of the aliens and transforms him from a man to the now-famous "starchild," a product of man and the aliens who is sent back to Earth to watch from space over his native planet. At what time in Earth's history the starchild appears is unimportant; the viewer can choose any convenient and personally satisfying point in our history.

Besides being an exhaustive exercise in searching out "theme and meaning," *2001: A Space Odyssey* is a work of great visual acuity. It is an experience in the poetry of motion. We are treated to vehicles dancing through space to the "Blue Danube Waltz." And thanks to the skillful hand of Kubrick the editor, magnificently composed and framed shots are compounded by a striking scene-to-scene flow rare in the mass manufacture of modernday film. Indeed, the jump-cut—from the man-ape tossing his bone-weapon heavenward in slow motion, to a spaceship ushering in the "Blue Danube Waltz"— remains one of the most breathtaking and inspired cuts in film history. The special effects and art direction—almost universally praised—are, in fact, overrated. Although nothing in terms of the film's Cinerama size had ever been attempted with similarly complicated effects, films such as *Forbidden Planet, This Island Earth,* and Disney's fanciful *Darby O'Gill and the Little People* are much more slick and much less obvious. Still, the special effects—although an end in themselves when one evaluates the film's magnificent box-office appeal—are rightly subservient to the theme.

Some of the props and stars from Thunderbirds Are Go!

Roy Thinnes (left) and Pat Wymark discuss the possibility of there being an earth-like planet in our orbit, but on the other side of the sun. From Journey to the Far Side of the Sun.

Gene Hackman (left) and Arthur Hill in Marooned.

123

Jerry Lewis (left), Janet Leigh, and Howard Morris as astronauts in Way . . . Way Out.

In light of the innovations fathered by *2001: A Space Odyssey,* it is not difficult to appreciate how most space films that followed seem—and are—anemic. A prime example is *Marooned* (1970), one of the silliest science-fiction films. This one has a trio of astronauts stranded in space after attempting to return home from a stay in space station *Ironman One.* Their retro-rockets have failed, so a miscast David Janssen hops aboard a shuttlecraft, which NASA just happened to have lying around, takes off for space during a hurricane, through whose eye he launches himself, and rescues two of the three spacemen (one has died) from Russian baddies who have also come upon the men. The special effects are two-dimensional, as are the characters, plot, and acting.

Countdown (1968), at least, makes no bones about being anything more than a modest moon-race effort. It features, coincidentally, future *Godfather* co-stars James Caan and Robert DuVall.

One highly creditable post-Kubrick space film was *Journey to the Far Side of the Sun* (1968), with special effects that on occasion, outshine those of *2001: A Space Odyssey.* (The miniatures, for example, are flawless.) This is the story of an astronaut who leaves Earth and lands on a planet in exactly the same orbit as our world, but the opposite side of the sun, hidden at all times from our telescopes. Roy Thinnes rockets to this world and discovers—after a period in which he thinks he has crash landed on his own world—that the two planets are similar down to the finest detail. The only difference is that the inhabitants drive on the opposite side of the road from earthlings, write backward, and so forth.

Astronaut Paul Mantee drops in on Adam West (TV's Batman) as the pair circles Mars. From Robinson Crusoe on Mars.

Vic Lundin pleads with Paul Mantee not to return him to his cruel alien masters. From Robinson Crusoe on Mars.

The magnificent airship
Albatross *from* Master of the
World.

One of the menaces faced and
overcome by John Agar in
Journey to the Seventh Planet.

The planet-roving vehicle in the Russian-made Voyage to a Pre-Historic Planet.

After many personal and scientific disasters on this other world, Thinnes heads for space in an attempt to rejoin the orbiting mother ship and return to Earth. Unfortunately, the extraterrestrial ship in which he goes into space has a polarity opposite from that of the mother ship, which rejects the new arrival. The astronaut's vehicle plummets back to Earth —destroying the space complex when Thinnes attempts to make a landing and igniting the spectacular scenes of explosive fury.

The picture attempts to kindle a profundity similar to that of *2001: A Space Odyssey* in its abstract philosophizing about the dichotomy of dual worlds, but it fails with a combination of meat-and-potatoes science fiction and quasi-profound themes. Neither a kid's film nor a cult film, the picture found a small, unprofitable audience in the middle. But although the work is an incohesive whole, the elements that comprise the finished effort are more than individually successful.

Thunderbirds Are Go! (1966) and *Thunderbird Six* (1968)—products of the Anderson team that did *Journey to the Far Side of the Sun,* as well as the TV series *UFO*—have been far more exploitable kiddie-matinee features. Based on the TV series *Thunderbirds* and featuring marionettes rather than real people (surprisingly, not one reviewer accused the actors of being wooden), the films are a marvel to behold, with a firm grip on the juvenile audience for which they were intended.

Way, Way Out (1966) is a heavy-handed effort featuring Jerry Lewis and Janet Leigh as American astronauts. For a year, they are sole inhabitants of a lunar weather station.

Edward Judd and Lionel Jeffries go romping about the surface of the moon, garbed in underwater pressure suits. From First Men in the Moon.

Edward Judd knocks Lionel Jeffries from his line of fire as the former prepares to kill the moon's ruler, the Grand Lunar. From First Men in the Moon.

Beneath the surface of the moon, Lionel Jeffries and Edward Judd find breathable air and strange vegetation. From First Men in the Moon.

The original ad art for First Men in the Moon.

There are some clever bits in the film, such as Lewis and his Russian counterpart getting drunk on Vodka pills, but there is also some awful dialogue ("This is where the fertilizer hits the ventilator," cries a despondent administrator). The fight between Lewis and the Russian—both drunk—in spacesuits on the moon's surface is not the clever sequence it could have been, and the film plods along incessantly.

Yet not even in this class is Don Knotts' *Reluctant Astronaut,* which came to us in 1968. Like *The Incredible Mr. Limpet* (1964), Knotts' earlier effort for Arthur Lubin (director of the 1943 *Phantom of the Opera),* this film is a juvenile fantasy. *Mouse on the Moon* (1963) had the Grand Duchy of Fenwick blasting off the moon in a rocket powered by Fenwickian wine. Not up to *The Mouse That Roared* (1959), *Mouse on the Moon* had, to its credit, fine performances by Margaret Rutherford and Terry-Thomas.

An excellent and offbeat ride through space was undertaken by George Pal and director Byron Haskin in *Robinson Crusoe on Mars* (1964), a clever and thoroughly convincing retelling of the classic tale. In the film, astronauts Paul Mantee and Adam West (before *Batman*) bail from their stricken spaceship to the Martian surface when their orbiting craft is crippled by an asteroid. West is killed upon impact, but Mantee and pet monkey Mona survive. How the Earthman finds food, water, and oxygen on the barren Martian surface is engrossing, the logic behind the film is reasonable, and the arrival of his man Friday—an escaped alien slave (being pursued by possessive aliens in saucers reminiscent of, if less convincing than, Pal's *War of the World* ships)—makes the story complete. The picture was filmed in Death Valley, over whose angry terrain were superimposed an impressive red-orange sky and flaming fireballs that swoop over the Martian surface in answer to flame geysers that dot the landscape. And the finale—the heroes' arrival at the Martian polar ice cap—is a sight to behold.

The Green Slime *attacks Robert Horton, in the film of the same name.*

A spaceport sequence from Moon Zero Two.

One of the splendid miniatures from First Spaceship on Venus, filmed in Totalvision, and starring Yoko Tani and Oldrick Lukes.

James Olson and Catherina Von Schell as Kemp and Clementine from Moon Zero Two.

A lunar shootout between good guys and bad guys in the first space Western. From Moon Zero Two.

Special effects are the star of *Journey to the Seventh Planet* (1960), in which John Agar and a crew of four land on Uranus, a world ruled—although this is supposed to be a secret —by a giant, all-knowing, illusion-creating brain. The crew encounters many unique and terrifying obstacles, such as a giant (stop-motion animation) prehistoric monster, some beautiful Earth girls (formulated by the brain, naturally), and a barrier of solidified energy that separates the astronauts from the brain. After much to-do, the spacemen pierce the barrier and freeze the brain with liquid oxygen. The film has fine production values and suffers only from a middling script and lukewarm acting.

If *Journey to the Seventh Planet* was merely average, the foreign import was better than *Valley of the Dragons* (1961), an adaptation of Jules Verne's classic *Off on a Comet.* This trite work features Cesare Danova (after the actor lost the role of *Ben-Hur* to Charlton Heston) and his companion—a man he was about to duel—swept from the Earth to the surface of a comet that passes our world every now and then. Once on the comet, the Earthmen encounter the most impressive collection of stock footage from (again!) *One Million B.C.* ever assembled. Not a single additional dinosaur sequence was filmed for the picture—a picture composed primarily of prehistoric settings. Even the makeup for the cavemen—one of the film's few budgetary expenditures—is poor. Naturally, our heroes stumble into a tribal war between the cave people and the river people. . . .

Another stab at Jules Verne was taken by Vincent Price as Robur the Conqueror in the special-effects-ful *Master of the World* (1961). Robur did not reach space, but speared the upper reaches of the atmosphere in his sky ship *Albatross,* in the company of such featured stalwarts as Henry Hull and Charles Bronson.

Americans were treated to a fine Soviet film, *Voyage to a Prehistoric Planet,* in 1964. Originally released as *Storm Planet, Voyage to a Prehistoric Planet* is another foreign film weakened by scenes filmed in the United States. These additional segments feature Basil Rathbone and Faith Domergue (the star of *It Came from Beneath the Sea*) as the liaison between a space station orbiting the moon and the first spaceship to attempt a landing on Venus. As the opening narration explains it,

The year: 2020. The moon has been explored and colonized, and the next space goal is about to be reached. The first landing by man on the planet Venus. Scientists profoundly hope that life similar to that on Earth may be found on this planet where so many physical conditions are like our own. Three rocketships of an international space expedition—the *Sirius, Vega,* and *Capella*—after having successfully traveled two hundred million miles, are in the final stages of their journey, rapidly approaching their destination.

No attempt is made to mingle the American actors with the Soviet originals; Domergue is in the mother ship orbiting Venus throughout the film, and Rathbone is in orbit around the moon. The astronauts who descend to the planet's surface in a shuttlecraft never appear with their orbiting lady friend.

The film was made with meticulous care, a cornerstone of Soviet film production. As with the earlier Soviet film *The Sword and the Dragon* (1959) (seen in the United States on a double bill with *Frankenstein 1970*), this film is mounted in lavish style, has excellent production values, and features carefully executed special effects. The other-worldliness of Venus was vividly and eerily reconstructed in a Soviet studio. The travelers journey about in a land-water-submarine vehicle with the guidance of a large, computerlike robot who is their companion and, quite often, their savior. A major flaw in the American release, however, is the dubbing. Technically, it is fine enough, but somehow the original Russian phrases, which must sound convincing in Russian, do not hold up at all well in English. The following exchange is an example.

COSMONAUT 1: *Capella,* sir—I'm afraid she's been hit by a meteorite.
COSMONAUT 2: Damn it!
COSMONAUT 1: Completely destroyed, sir.
COSMONAUT 2: And almost to their goal. It seems so unfair.
COSMONAUT 1: There's no fair or unfair to a meteorite. You get hit . . . you die.

At this point in the conversation, mediocrity takes full reign as Rathbone, aboard the *Luna-7* space station, comes over the radio with, "We were deeply shocked to learn of the loss of the *Capella.* Flight Plan A, however, must still be followed." Rathbone is the epitome of sensitivity, expressing such sincere regret at the loss of a ship and its crew of six.

One of the magnificent sets of the incredibly vast spaceship carrying passengers on a Voyage to the End of the Universe.

A particularly successful film was *First Men in the Moon* (1965), starring Lionel Jeffries and Edward Judd, who, through the courtesy of Ray Harryhausen, go to the moon in the late nineteenth century and discover monstrous moon calves and equally loathesome Selenites.

En route, the pair most likely passed the space station inhabited by *The Green Slime,* a 1969 film featuring men in monster suits posing as the galactic glop and looking not unlike rejects from the *Voyage to the Bottom of the Sea* TV series. The acting is bad, the script is inane, and the sets are as cheap as they come. Star Robert Horton (of TV's *Man Called Shenandoah*) looks sturdy but isn't really. Only the color in *Green Slime* is good—although for completists, the Slime is actually not green, but blue. Somehow, though, *The Blue Slime* just doesn't have that ring to it. . . .

A better film is *Mutiny in Outer Space* (1965), a grade-B movie wherein Earthmen exploring another planet accidentally carry a weird, funguslike growth back to space station X-7. Before long the monster has grown and, in several stop-motion animation sequences, takes over the entire space station. Comparison with *The Green Slime* is inevitable, though hardly something to which one might look forward. Whereas the Green Slime throve on energy and could grow to the size of a man in less than a minute, the fungus in *Mutiny in Outer Space* drew sustenance from the atmosphere of the ship itself.

Two formidable film talents came up with minor, unconvincing efforts in the genre—Walt Disney gave us Tom Tryon as *The Moon Pilot* (1960), a colorful, empty-headed little film, and Bob Hope and Bing Crosby took a trip in 1962 to the planet Plutonium in a mildly diverting effort known as *Road to Hong Kong*.

Spaceflight IC-1 (1965) was a low-grade journey into deep space that fell prey to a routine script, and "blood rust," repulsive man-eating blobs returned to earth on an American space probe, was the protagonist in a minor 1968 adventure, *Spacemaster X-7*. Then there was *Moon Zero Two* (1969), starring James Olson (*Andromeda Strain*) and Adrienne Cori (*A Clockwork Orange*). *Moon Zero Two* was accurately billed as the first space-Western, featuring ray guns instead of six-shooters, rocketships instead of horses, and a leading lady known as Clementine.

Films featuring men in space continued to come from abroad. *Twelve to the Moon* (1960) is routine international silliness wherein a team of spacemen from different countries make it to the moon. The effects are passable, but the acting is not. The story centers around a character known as the Great Coordinator, a being that dwells within the moon, whence it draws heat from the Earth's atmosphere.

First Spaceship on Venus (1960) is a German film with an international cast, set in the 1980s. The film has fine special effects but was badly butchered for American release. This, in addition to awkward dubbing, makes the picture difficult to follow. Conversely, a Czechoslovakian film entitled *Ikaria XB1* (1964) has incredible impact, despite emasculation before being shown here as *Voyage to the End of the Universe*. The film details a trip through space wherein the spacious, attractively mounted trappings of an immense starship call harsh attention to the small human beings within. There is a lot of brooding philosophy in the film; yet despite the everpresent plague of dubbing, the charm and class of this production are quite impressive. If one can see past the film's nihilistic attitude, *Voyage to the End of the Universe* comes across as a remarkable film.

The story of Frank Chapman merits our attention; it is he who, in the 1980s, makes a trip to *The Phantom Planet*. This 1961 film is perhaps the last of the space films to bear all the trappings of the fifties. The acting, sets, plot, and dialogue are simple minded but not offensively juvenile, and the film is charmingly naïve. Captain Chapman (Dean Fredericks) wings aloft to discover why American rockets are disappearing. While flitting about the stars, Chapman's ship is pulled to the surface of an asteroid; leaving his vehicle, the spaceman steps onto the surface of this strange, barren world . . . and passes out. When he awakens, he is four inches tall. Chapman soon discovers the atmosphere of this planetoid—Rheton, to the natives—is conducive to such oddities, and during the course of the film, Chapman helps the Rhetonians conquer the warlike monster Solarites and is returned, eventually, to normal size by the little oxygen remaining in his spacesuit air tanks. The small, jet-propelled world (Rheton flits about the solar system, its own rocket ship) returns Chapman to a point where he can be rescued by a passing spaceship. The film is innocent fun. A superfluous commodity for the new sixties breed of filmgoer, *The Phantom Planet* school closed its doors for good.

Mama Gorgo levels London in search of her captured offspring. From Gorgo.

Baby Gorgo attacks a diving bell containing a pair of intrepid adventurers. From Gorgo.

MONSTERS ON THE LOOSE

Monsters on the loose comprise one genre that did not change radically from the fifties to the sixties. What did happen was that the production center for these epics shifted from Hollywood to Japan, which now owns the market. Before we delve into the various resurrections of Godzilla and others, let's look at some of the more original efforts in the field.

Gorgo (1962), a high-budget film from Great Britain, is certainly one of the finer efforts of this sort. Indeed, *Gorgo* is everything *The Giant Behemoth* (1958) could—and should—have been. The story is routine enough. Underwater volcanic activity awakens an ages-old monster from hibernation. Two down-and-out seamen capture the beast and, on their freighter, transport Gorgo to London, where the creature is put on exhibit in a circus. Things go well for the entrepreneurs until the monster's mother—four times the size of her gargantuan infant—decimates London in search of her imprisoned child. Reunited, the two return to the sea, leaving mankind a bit dazed but wiser for the experience.

Star Bill Travers, later to gain fame as the human lead in *Born Free* (1966), is quite good as the ship captain who captures the beast. All the supporting actors are sincere and, if anything, tend to underplay, which in this sort of film is far better than doing it straight. There is a great feel for British locale in *Gorgo*, and all the English landmarks are mercilessly leveled before the last reel has run its course. The special effects are superb, and Gorgo is tactfully kept in shadow throughout most of the film, which enhances the mood while making the special effects that much less obvious.

Reptilicus, the monster pulled from the bottom of an oil well, ravages Copenhagen.

Mothra wings her wi way on a destruc swath over Ja

Another British entry in the field is *Konga*. This 1961 film wastes the considerable talents of Michael Gough as a scientist who discovers a serum in the African jungle that, when injected into the bloodstream of an ape, causes the animal to grow. Gough then uses a gorilla-sized chimpanzee to help him win the attention of a female student by eliminating rival suitors. Things get out of hand when Gough's jealous wife injects Konga with a dosage that causes the ape to grow to the height of fifty feet.

Off-screen, Konga is nothing more than a man in an ape suit, but some creditable miniature sets highlight the monster's rampage of London. Only when the enormous simian picks up Gough, à la *King Kong* and Fay Wray, does the absurdity of the situation become unbearable, especially when Gough cries, "Konga . . . Konga . . . put me down! Put me down, I say!" The giant ape is finally shot to death by the police and, in classical form, reverts to his natural chimp size upon death.

138

Reptilicus (1961) is another film in which a dormant monster is awakened by man's tomfoolery—in this instance, men drilling for oil—and runs madly through city streets trampling people underfoot. The acting, dubbing, plot, and special effects are all scraped from the bottom of the barrel, and in the end, though Reptilicus is blown to pieces, each piece threatens to grow into a new monster. The film did not do well enough to merit a sequel.

Incidentally, *Gorgo, Konga,* and *Reptilicus* were all turned into sex novels by Monarch Books. In *Konga,* the professor gets the girl . . . and one *has* to read *Reptilicus* to find out what the man who discovers Reptilicus has to do with a female former tight-rope walker. The films are better, if less interesting.

Japan had already introduced Godzilla and Rodan to the public in the mid- to late fifties, and it was time for the rest of the soon-to-be-familiar entourage to make its debut. From Toho—the undisputed champs of the monster epic and creators of Godzilla and Rodan—came a surprisingly good film entitled *Mothra* (1962), in which a giant caterpillar follows two six-inch-tall girls to Japan after the pair was kidnapped from the monster's Pacific island by a greedy impresario. After leveling a large portion of Japan, Mothra halves the Tokyo Tower and, using it for support, spins a cocoon. Days later, the monster emerges a full-grown moth and annihilates portions of the city left standing on her previous tour of destruction.

Godzilla, Rodan, and (in the lower right-hand corner) Mothra battle Ghidrah, The Three Headed Monster.

The film is loaded with charm, expertise, and maturity. There is something very Japanese about the monster Mothra, an element missing in Godzilla and Rodan. Mothra is a delicate creature, despite her size and destructive powers, a monster without malice, seeking to regain only what is rightfully hers. The colors and carriage of Mothra are not unlike the designs on classical Japanese kites with their weightless beauty. In the end, of course, the girls are returned to Mothra, and the three return to their Pacific home.

Mothra returned on several occasions to do battle with monsters. The first command engagement was a bout with Godzilla in a film called *Godzilla vs. the Thing* (1964), in which Mothra is the Thing. In this effort, a sorry finale finds Mothra lifting Godzilla by the tail and dumping the fifty-ton dinosaur into the ocean because the reptile was menacing Mothra's egg.

Mothra came back, this time with Rodan and Godzilla, in an impressive epic *Ghidrah, the Three-Headed Monster* (1965), Ghidrah being a multiheaded, fire-breathing dragon. What

Godzilla prepares to do battle with Mothra in Godzilla vs. the Thing.

elevates this adventure above the rest is the quality of its special effects. Ghidrah is born in a flaming fireball that shoots skyward from the creature's gargantuan egg, an awesome spectacle to behold. But Ghidrah is done in, for the nonce, when Godzilla, Rodan, and Mothra gang up on him.

It was Ghidrah versus Godzilla and Rodan in *Monster Zero* (1970), in which aliens from space borrow Godzilla and Rodan from Earth to combat Ghidrah, who is ravaging their home planet.

In *Godzilla vs. the Sea Monster* (1966), Godzilla does it solo against a slithery monster-lobster on a remote Pacific island.

Son of Godzilla (1968) introduces Godzilla's little boy, Minya, a monster that, unlike his father, cannot exhale radioactive fire; he can muster only enough heat for a smoke ring or two. During the film, Godzilla and son battle a trio of giant praying mantises, but the effort is played strictly for laughs.

King Kong vs. Godzilla (1963) marked the return of the famous ape—no longer a stop-motion model, but a man in a monkey suit—who does battle with Godzilla in Tokyo after being shipped there under sedation by boat. If you saw the film in the United States, Kong won; if you saw it in Japan, Godzilla won. In either case, the audience lost.

Kong returned for *King Kong Escapes* (1967), the story of a Communist power that erects a giant mechanical Kong to dig for a nuclear ore in the Arctic. On another front, American submarine commander Rhodes Reason and his Japanese crew land on Kong's island, and the ape finds them just as they are about to be inhospitably trounced by a rubbery-looking tyrannosaurus. Naturally, Kong and the mechani-Kong meet and do battle. Aside from the mechanical robot, this film is a remake of the original *King Kong,* and it's not bad, technically. The acting and dubbing are, as usual, abysmal, but the quality of the special effects more than compensates for this failing.

Perhaps the most wild and woolly of all the Japanese monster films produced by Toho is *Destroy All Monsters* (1969), a free-for-all who's who of Toho monsterdom. In this film, Ghidrah is returned to Earth by a group of Japanese-looking aliens known as the Kilaks, who are able to turn from people to rocks at a moment's notice (for camouflage). The Kilaks have established a base in space, from which they plan to invade Earth.

Meanwhile, all the monsters of the world now live on Monster Island, a place where the misunderstood Godzilla and others can find contentment away from humanity's wicked presence. All this time, it appears, the monsters were really "good guys," pleading only for acceptance. The Kilaks come to Earth and set up a device that actually turns the monsters bad. The Kilaks free the beasts from Monster Island, and the dinosaurs ravage the world. Earth is finally saved by the destruction of the Kilak forces by Japanese astronauts and the subsequent release of the good monsters from Kilak control.

But as icing on the cake, the Kilaks had brought Ghidrah to Earth to expedite its destruction, and Ghidrah is an inherently wicked creature. So the beast has to be subdued. Out from under the Kilak spell, the monsters unite to battle Ghidrah. The scorecard reads, Godzilla, Rodan, Anzilla, Mothra, Aspiga (a giant spider), Manda (a giant snake), and Minya versus Ghidrah. Ghidrah loses, and the monsters return to Monster Island, content and waving goodbye to the camera.

Monster Island figured prominently in my favorite Godzilla sequel, *Godzilla's Revenge* (1970), a modern morality tale composed primarily of stock footage from previous monsteramas. The star of *Godzilla's Revenge* is a lovable little kid. He is laughed at by his school chums because he is constantly dreaming of being in exotic places (especially Monster Island). Whenever the boy dreams, he visits Monster Island and plays games with Minya. Here is how the film weaves its story.

STEWARDESS: Welcome aboard Pan Am flight one, direct to Monster Island. We'll be flying at thirty-five thousand feet and will arrive on schedule. We hope you have a pleasant flight.

PILOT: Monster Island. We are ready to land!

The plane lands, and our hero disembarks.

Godzilla and Rodan are transported to another planet to do battle with Ghidrah in Monster Zero.

LAD: There's Gamakera (a giant spider)! There's Bosaurus! There's Manda! Anguilla! And golly, look at that! (*as a giant vulture swoops at* GODZILLA *and is fried by the monster's radioactive breath*)! Oh, hi, Minya!

MINYA: Hi! Come on over here! I won't hurt ya!

LAD: You won't?

MINYA: No! Don't be afraid. Why'd you come here?

LAD: I wanted to see you!

MINYA: Hmmm. . .yer folks'll get kinda worried, won't they?

LAD: I don't think so. They're hardly home any time at all.

MINYA: Ohhh . . . (*Knowingly, realizing that Kenji escapes to Monster Island because he hasn't parents concerned enough to sacrifice a few hours at the factory in order to be home with their son*).

Back in Japan, the boy becomes involved with bank robbers when he recognizes them. They kidnap him, but it all works out for the best. When the boy escapes and the convicts are caught, the youngster's parents realize how they've been neglecting him.

The film is intentionally juvenile and as such is fine entertainment. When Minya is forced to battle a monster twenty times his size, the effect on the boy is pronounced; this example gives him the inner strength to battle his own enemies—bullies and bank robbers.

Godzilla's Revenge is better, by far, than most of the Saturday-morning TV cartoon tripe.

Toho wasn't the only one to see the dollar signs on the wall and raise long-lost monsters from the dead. Others made films such as *Gappa, the Triphibian Monster* (1968), wherein a pair of beaked dinosaurs rise from the ocean and level Japan; *Varan the Unbelievable*

A space station featured in the
giant-walrus-on-the-loose
monster film known as Gorath.

(1960), featuring a supernatural dinosaur from the bottom of a bottomless lake; and *War of the Gargantuas* (1970), featuring Russ Tamblyn as a scientist trying to help a hairy giant who has a murderous twin brother (one is brown, the other green, for easy identification); and *Gorath* (1962), featuring a giant walrus. . . .

One other monster that made a great impact on both Japanese and American audiences, although nowhere near the impression made by Godzilla and Company, was a giant turtle known as Gamera. This monster, when he withdrew head and feet into his shell, spouted fire and zipped through sky and space, spinning wildly.

The first film in the series entitled, simply enough, *Gamera* (1965), saw the monster *completely* level Japan. No weapon on Earth could stop the titanic tortoise. Thus, in a clever—if rather contrived—conclusion, the creature is lured into the nose cone of a rocket and sent to Mars.

In true monster fashion, the creature returns to Earth in *Gamera vs. Monster X* (1966), to do battle with one of the most absurd monsters ever, a large spiked creature that exhales spears the way Godzilla breathes radioactive fire. Indeed, at one point the mutated stegosaurus spears Gamera's neck, legs, and tail, making it impossible for the creature to withdraw into his shell and fly away. Then, adding insult to injury, the monster pushes Gamera onto his back.

144

King Kong goes on a destructive rampage in King Kong vs. Godzilla.

After this poignant monster mess came *Gamera vs. Viras* (1967), a starfish-like space creature; *Gamera vs. Gaos* (1968), a flying monster; *Gamera vs. Guiron,* Guiron being a giant living knife with arms; and finally, *Gamara vs. Leoman* (1971), another prehistoric fun fest.

Even Frankenstein's monster made an appearance in a disaster called *Frankenstein Conquers the World* (1966), in which a young child found after the Hiroshima blast grows to monstrous size and battles a giant lizard monster, saving the world. The special effects, makeup, and acting—by the late Nick Adams, who also appeared in *Monster Zero*—are all grade Z.

The subterranean Morlocks, lords of the future. From The Time Machine.

Yvette Mimieux in the grip of a Morlock. From The Time Machine.

A rare shot of the sphinx-head entrance to the underground domain of the Morlocks. From The Time Machine.

Rod Taylor, as George the Time Traveler, in The Time Machine.

A view of the life-size mock-up of the Blood Vessel from Fantastic Voyage.

The hemonauts grow from small to tall after their Fantastic Voyage through the human body.

TRIPS THROUGH TIME AND OTHER DIMENSIONS

George Pal got the sixties off to a rip-roaring start—as he had the fifties—with his beautifully made, big-box-office film *The Time Machine* (1960). Returning to H. G. Wells for source material, Pal and the special-effects wizardry of Jim Danforth, Tim Barr, Wah Chang, and Gene Warren take Rod Taylor from the year 1900 to a time seven thousand years in the future and a world peopled by the Eloi—a submissive race of fair-haired, fair-skinned human beings—and the cruel mutant master Morlocks, apelike creatures that breed the Eloi for food. Taylor falls in love with one of the Eloi—Yvette Mimieux—and when she is taken to the underground cavern of the Morlocks to meet her fate, Taylor leads the Eloi in a rebellion that ends with destruction of the Morlocks in a series of fantastic explosions.

Despite solid acting and an above-average script, the Oscar-winning special effects are the film's real star, and the sequences wherein Taylor whips through time—slowly, at first, then faster, watching candles melt, flowers bloom, and days pass in seconds—are astounding. Taylor stops several times, first during World War I and then in the midst of an atomic war in 1966. During this war an explosion rips open the Earth and Taylor returns to his machine just as it is engulfed by hot lava. The molten rock solidifies around the machine as Taylor jumps into the far future. Finally, after centuries of rain and sand have eroded the mountain, Taylor finds himself once more in sunlight, in the world of the Eloi. The film's use of time and its fantasizing about the mysteries of travel through that dimension are creditable, and the entire film is fun all the way.

147

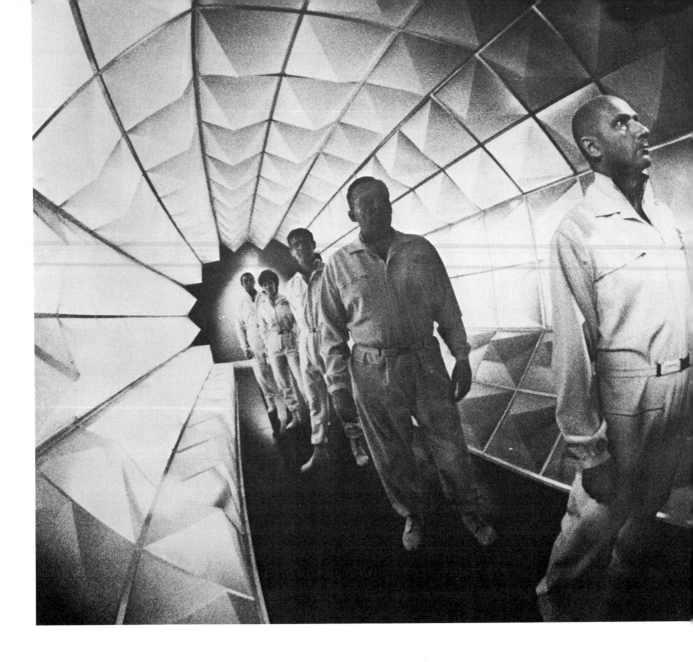

Certainly the most unusual voyage, if one of the least satisfying, aesthetically, is *Fantastic Voyage* (1966), one of the more overrated science-fiction pictures. The film has exquisite sets and art direction, but the acting, process photography, and optical effects are thoroughly disappointing. The plot follows five scientists who, along with a sleek and interesting submarine, are shrunk to microscopic size and injected into the bloodstream of a leading scientist who has a brain clot inaccessible through surgical means. Despite the presence of a saboteur—Donald Pleasance—Raquel Welch, Stephen Boyd, and company succeed in their goal. Pleasance is devoured by a white blood cell—a fitting demise for a red blood cell—and the hemonauts lose their craft to defensive body agents. In a contrived and unnecessary finale, the travelers begin to expand, their time used up, while they are still in the anesthetized scientist's head. They barely manage to escape in a teardrop before exiting the hard way.

The human organs through which the actors move are life-sized sets reconstructed in great detail with amazing artistry. Unfortunately, scenes of the craft sailing through the

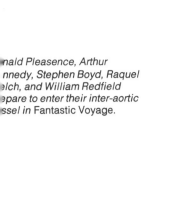

Raquel Welch and Arthur
Kennedy prepare to blast a blood
clot in the body of a wounded
scientist. From Fantastic Voyage.

body, sequences of the shrinking and growing of the scientists, and similar effects work
are not at all convincing.

One film that is a classic is the 1968 Franklin Schaffner epic *Planet of the Apes.* Mr.
Schaffner had worked with *Apes* star Charlton Heston previously on *The Warlord* (1965),
and after *Apes* he went on to direct such superb films as *Patton* (1970) and *Nicholas and
Alexandra* (1972). Schaffner's ability to focus on the human element in the face of
awesome spectacle is one of his greatest assets. Despite the fantastic setting of the
Grand Canyon, the ape city, and panoramas of long, sprawling terrain, the camera never
loses sight of its main character, Heston, who portrays Taylor, commander of a flight of
two other men and one woman into space. The woman is killed during the flight—they are
all in suspended animation, and her hibernatory mechanism fails.

The three surviving astronauts leave their stricken ship when it crashes on an alien world,
and they soon discover that it is a planet in which the apes, capable of speech and

149

John Phillip Law and Jane Fonda
in Barbarella.

Charlton Heston descends from a mountain peak in Planet of the Apes.

thought, are the masters and man the hunted animal. Of Heston's two companions, one is stuffed and placed in a museum, and the other is lobotomized. Heston is caged, but he escapes with the help of two friendly chimpanzees named Zira and Cornelius (Kim Hunter and Roddy McDowall). After a series of literate and beautifully allegorical sequences, astronaut Heston discovers that this is not some alien world, but Earth in the year 3978. The scene in which Heston stumbles upon the remains of the Statue of Liberty, her upraised torch stabbing through the vast expanse of beach on which he is traveling, is not easily forgotten.

The film makes a shambles of the book by Pierre Boulle, playing down the plot and emphasizing, often to an uncomfortable degree, the philosophy and symbolism. The sequence wherein Heston, on trial, is greeted by a jury of three apes in a see-no-evil, hear-no-evil, speak-no-evil pose is a bit much. But Heston turns in a magnificent performance, and as apes, Hunter, McDowall, and Maurice Evans—all of whom repeat in later sequels—are wholly convincing.

The much-lauded makeup of John Chambers is not especially impressive. It lacks the texture, quality, and character of, for example, earlier Jack Pierce work for the Universal

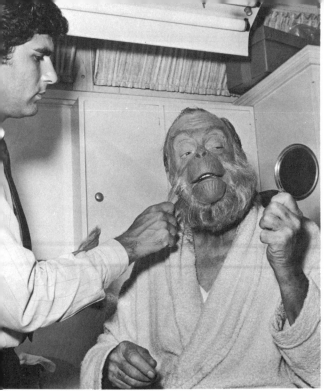

After a hard day's shooting, Maurice Evans is only too happy to doff his Planet of the Apes *Dr. Zaius make-up.*

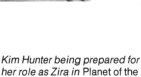

Kim Hunter being prepared for her role as Zira in Planet of the Apes.

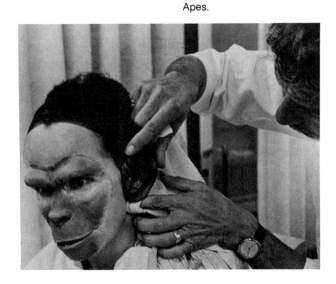

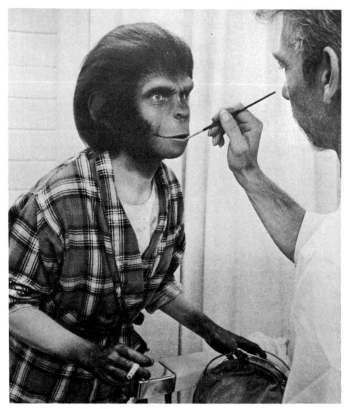

films of the thirites and forties. Pierce, lacking the advanced tools and techniques of today, painted a more articulate tapestry with his grainy, sweltering faces, such as Karloff's Frankenstein and Mummy and Chaney's Wolf Man. The Chambers work, though convincing, is mass produced, prepackaged, and lacking in warmth.

On the other hand, the set direction—of spaceship and ape city—is marvelous, the photography generally superb, and the second-unit stunt work exceptional. The scenes of Heston racing through the cavelike ape city pursued by apes on horseback are breathtaking.

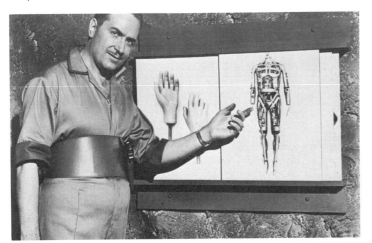

Forrest J. Ackerman as a robotics expert in The Time Travelers.

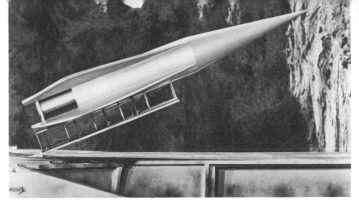

The ship that will carry normal human beings away from the mutants of future earth. Its destination: The Andromeda Galaxy. From The Time Travelers.

Still on earth, but in the present, is Kerwin Mathews—alumnus of *Seventh Voyage of Sinbad* (1958), *Jack the Giant Killer* (1962), *Boy Who Cried Werewolf* (1973), and others—who does battle with the Red Chinese in *Battle Beneath the Earth* (1968). Despite ray guns and sparks galore, this film is a wholly unconvincing disappointment. Mathews is a wooden actor, but he is an honest performer, and in most of his roles, the ex school teacher has done an admirable job. As a psychic investigator in the TV pilot *Ghost Breaker* (never sold, but the best of the television ghost-investigator efforts) he was perfect, his hair streaked with gray and his carriage aloof and determined. In *Battle Beneath the Earth,* he does cut a fine figure of an army officer . . . until he opens his mouth. Then he sounds like an actual army officer attempting to act.

Just as poor as *Battle beneath the Earth* is a minor effort entitled *Around the World under the Sea* (1966), directed by former second-unit director Andrew Marton. This movie was a water-logged quickie for sea veteran Lloyd Bridges and U.N.C.L.E. alumnus David McCallum. It tells of a voyage to plant sonar devices along faults in the Earth's undersea crust to serve as warning devices for earthquakes and tidal waves. Traveling at great depths, the hydronauts encounter a volcano and a monster eel. But even these minor diversions are not quite enough to relieve the boredom.

Time travel, after Pal's initial effort in the sixties, was a popular theme. Robert Clarke visited the year 2024 in *Beyond the Time Barrier* (1960). As in *World without End,* the Earthman of the present helps an underground race of the future overcome surface mutants, turned from men to monster by an atomic war in the year 1971. *Dimension Five* (1968) features Jeffrey Hunter as a U.S. agent of the future who journeys to the present and prevents a Chinese hydrogen bomb from destroying Los Angeles. On a less altruistic mission were a group of scientists known as *The Time Travelers* (1964) who voyage 107 years into the future via a time window, to find a world populated by subterranean humans, their androids, and—once again—angry, hostile mutants. Starving, the mutants storm the well-stocked human residence, the inhabitants of which then head for Alpha Centauri, some twenty-five trillion miles away, via photon-powered rockets. The audience heads for home in disgust.

Not through time, but through an incredible sphere of fantasy, move the featured players in a charming and impressive film from Czechoslovakia, *The Fabulous World of Jules Verne* (1961). In this live-action animation effort, the assistant to a kidnapped scientist pursues his mentor's shady abductors through the many fantasy worlds of Jules Verne. The animation was drawn to capture the mood, look, and feel of eighteenth- and nineteenth-century engravings. Done with care and expertise, this is a winning film all the way.

A pair of British films assembled from a television series features the character of Dr. Who —portrayed by Peter Cushing—who visits the world of the future, a world inhabited by

The Menoptera is one of the
beautiful butterfly creatures that
inhabits the world of Vortis . . .
until the uprising of the
subservient Zarbi. From the Dr.
Who TV series.

An army of the robot monsters.
From Dr. Who and the Daleks.

Maureen O'Brien with Koquillion
in The Powerful Enemy segment
of the BBC TV serial Dr. Who.
This being, from the planet Dido,
is only one of the many menaces
faced by the adventuresome
professor.

Scott Brady and Gigi Perreau in
Journey to the Center of Time.

creatures known as the Daleks. These are clumsy, robotized creatures that move about on little wheels set beneath their pyramid-shaped bodies. They plan evil doings from the shelter of their impregnable fortress—which, from underground, Cushing and his co-travelers penetrate. In *Dr. Who and the Daleks* (1965), Dr. Who arrives in the future with some family members thanks to his time-and-relative-dimension-in-space device. He helps the Thals, a peaceable people not unlike the Eloi in *Time Machine,* defeat the overlord Daleks.

But the Daleks return to enslave London in *Daleks: Invasion Earth 2150,* a 1966 feature in which the Daleks overcome and mesmerize Earthlings, ravaging the world from an enormous spaceship supported by *visible* wires. As one might expect, the Daleks are defeated once more by the irrepressible Dr. Who. Both adventures are lively entertainment, and had each been more expert in a technical and script capacity, the result would have been far more satisfying.

This holds true, as well, for *Journey to the Center of Time* (1967), a film starring Scott Brady of *Destination: Inner Space* (1966). In addition to needing a better script and more professional special effects, however, *Journey to the Center of Time* lacks solid acting, worthwhile sets, and a plot.

156

Barbara Eden, Peter Lorre, and
Walter Pidgeon in the feature film
Voyage to the Bottom of the Sea.

THE FUTURE OF MAN

What with the cold war and Cuban missile crisis, the end-of-the-world theme was a popular playground for filmmakers in the sixties. *Voyage to the Bottom of the Sea* (1961), based on a novel by Theodore Sturgeon, stars Walter Pidgeon as the intrepid commander of the submarine *Seaview*. Here is a race against time and hot-headed authorities to extinguish the Van Allen radiation belt, set ablaze by meteoric bombardment. Dousing the fire can be accomplished, claims Pidgeon, only by firing a missile into the belt from the North Pole. Of course, no one believes him. Despite protests from the United Nations and pursuit by navy submarines, the atom-powered *Seaview* manages to reach the pole, fire the weapon, and save the world.

Less fortunate were the principals of *Crack in the World* (1965), a tale about the firing of an atomic projectile into the center of the Earth to benefit mankind by releasing the Earth's interior energy. Dana Andrews is a scientist dying of radiation poisoning who wants to be remembered as a great man after his death. He has sponsored the project from the start and is fully responsible for the missile's detonation. Conversely, Kieran Moore is a scientist convinced that such a detonation will fully open an already dangerous crack in the Earth's crust.

Headquarters for the atomic missile launch that caused a Crack in the World.

Meanwhile, Andrews' wife—Moore's ex-lover and Andrews' ex-student—wants her husband to worry less about the project and to leave his mark on humankind by giving her a child. But for fear of side effects from his radiation poisoning, he will not.

In any event, the bomb goes off, and the Earth cracks as Moore said it would. An absurd love triangle—Moore still wants Andrews' wife—is put to the rear while humankind races desperately against time to stop the crack, which is moving along the ocean floor at three miles per hour, from encircling and cleaving the entire globe. The highlight of the film focuses on an attempt to stop the crack by exploding a nuclear bomb in the maw of a giant dormant volcano in the path of the fault, to provide a pressure valve for the rampant fissure. In order to detonate the weapon, the scientists carry it into the volcano crater, after being placed there by helicopter, and release the bomb. The result is spectacular. The volcano does indeed explode . . . but instead of stopping the crack, the men have succeeded only in altering its direction. And the cleft is now moving more rapidly than before.

The end product: A new moon, born when the Earth goes partially to pieces. Moore and Andrews' wife—who only respected Andrews but always loved Moore—are Earth's sole survivors, an Adam and Eve, to repopulate the world. The film is lavishly mounted and well acted, and it makes for solid entertainment.

Another interesting if not wholly successful effort is Val Guest's *Day the Earth Caught Fire* (1961). In this film simultaneous nuclear detonations by the United States and the Soviet Union throw the Earth off its rotational axis. What follows is interesting, though hardly illuminating. There are riots, a scarcity of supplies, rape, and so forth. In an effort to save the world, the two countries explode more bombs to right the Earth. The film ends with the explosion of the new devices, and we are left to speculate on the fate of the world.

The film has strong performances by Janet Munro (of *The Crawling Eye* and *Darby O'Gill and the Little People*) and Edward Judd (star of Harryhausen's *First Men in the Moon*). Though the movie is shot primarily in black and white, the scenes wherein the heat of the sun begins to fry our wandering planet are tinted a pale yellow. The film is at its best when it dwells on the people's reaction to the approaching doom and at its worst when it attempts to present the catastrophe in visual terms.

Not quite so good is Roger Corman's *Last Woman on Earth* (1961), a rather hopeless effort revolving around the last woman and two men left alive after a display of atomic might. More interesting is Ray Milland's little-seen *Panic in the Year Zero* (1962), a picture he directed and in which he starred. The film features one family and their efforts to survive in the mountains after a nuclear war. The world was far from obliterated by the atomic exchange, and Milland decided to move from urban Los Angeles to escape the potential danger of city life during the postwar unrest. Unfortunately, the film bogs down, not in plot or idea, both of which are fine, but in acting and directing. It suffers, as well, from static photography and a slow, pock-marked script. It does, however, make good use of location to evince the mood and feel of the situation and the family's isolation, with the threat of attack from human animals lurking behind every tree—is well explored. It could, however, have been much better.

More an art film—and one of the more brutal films involving postwar/potential-war activities is Joseph Losey's *These Are the Damned* (1965). The film is an intricate, initially

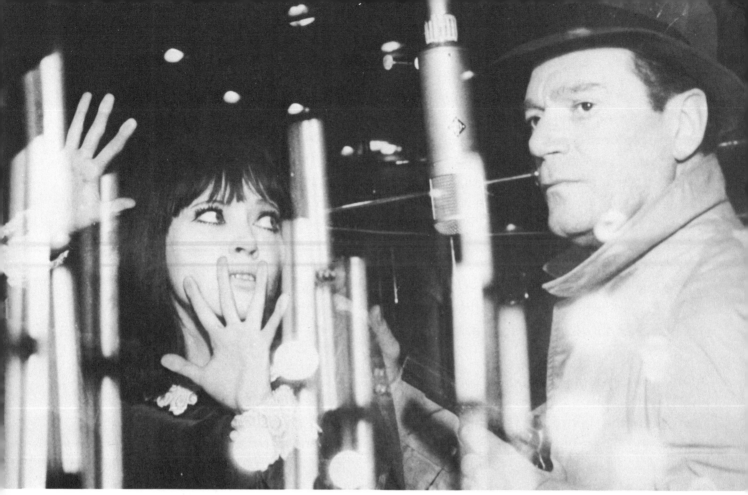

confusing work about youngsters who are the children of radiation-contaminated parents; these offspring are kept in a secluded retreat as potential parents of a future race of human beings in the event that the existing race is annihilated by atomic warfare. Sensing an injustice, MacDonald Carey and Shirley Anne Field free the children and, in the process are contaminated; all for naught, since the children are rounded up by their guardians and returned to captivity. It's a brutal, sterile world into which the children are being raised, and the film is stark, striking, and unrelenting in its pessimism.

Along the same lines is the more optimistic *Fahrenheit 451* (1966), a more blatant "art" film than most science fiction before it. This strangely poetic adaptation of Ray Bradbury's classic novel tells the story of a rebel book burner in an oppressive social clime where books are unlawful. The only way around this governmental edict is to commit the books to memory, which is what the principals do. The technical aspects of the film are far more impressive than its underplayed drama, and director François Truffaut works within his budgetary limitations to produce a film of admirable beauty and some impact.

Alphaville (1965) is another art-frilled production that is interesting in neither technique nor story. It is an overstated comic book done straight, with pseudo-intellectual touches. The film features a manhunt in a futuristic city, Alphaville, run by an electronic brain tagged Alpha-60. Sent to this city of logic and reason to secure a scientist named Von Braun, star detective Lemmy Caution (Eddie Constantine) is forced to kill his prey when the old fellow refuses to leave. Not content with this murder, Caution feeds Alpha-60 poetry—a medium it is unable to categorize or comprehend—and the great brain is

nna Karina and Eddie
onstantine in the futuristic city
phaville.

A confrontation at the North Pole
in Ice Station Zebra.

Patrick McGoohan (left) and Rock
Hudson in Ice Station Zebra.

*The war room in Dr. Strangelove.
George C. Scott is third from the
right.*

Peter Sellers as Lionel Mandrake,
a rather proper British officer from
Stanley Kubrick's magnificent
black comedy Dr. Strangelove.

A faulty human is attacked in
Creation of the Humanoi

destroyed. It is a sterile, technological world through which director Jean-Luc Godard's characters move, and the film is one of muddled meaning and even more pretentious style.

The Satan Bug (1965) is a talky film from John Sturges, who has given us a few great films and is certainly a capable technician. He fumbled *Marooned* (1970) and *Ice Station Zebra* (1968) but managed to make *something* out of *Satan Bug*. The Alistair MacLean novel on which the film is based is a difficult one for film, since there is less action in this work than in, for example, *Puppet on a Chain* (1972) or *Guns of Navarone* (1961). The Satan Bug is a deadly virus stolen from a top-secret lab, and the film details efforts made to retrieve the bug. Sturges manages to build a modicum of tension, but the film would have been far better at half its length. For comparison, *The Andromeda Strain* (1971), a similar effort by Robert Wise, is much better. But then, Wise is rarely off target, what with such films as *Day the Earth Stood Still* (1951), *West Side Story* (1960), and *Sound of Music* (1965) under his belt.

Fail Safe (1964) is the stuffy adaptation of the Eugene Burdick–Harvey Wheeler novel in which bombers pass a "fail-safe" border—a point beyond which the planes are to bomb Moscow and ignore orders to return, unless they come in a particular code over a particular channel. The special receiver malfunctions, and the planes actually bomb the Soviet Capital. The President of the United States, played with brooding indecision by Henry Fonda, is now obliged to bomb New York City, with no prior announcement, to prevent Soviet retaliation and a widening of the war.

The theme of *Fail Safe*—the fallibility of man and machine—is hammered home, but a sense of "we're only human" self-consciousness shrouds the film like a moral fog. This rather self-righteous cloud hides the real issue, which is not, as the film intimates, "How can we make the world safe when man is really such an idiotic creature?" but rather, "How can we make the world safe by working within man's limitations?"

Better by far than *Fail Safe* is Stanley Kubrick's pre–*2001: A Space Odyssey* effort, *Dr. Strangelove, or How I Learned to Stop Worrying and Love the Bomb* (1963). Using, again,

the idea of a fail-safe point and based on a pulp-oriented novel, *Red Alert,* by Peter Bryant, *Dr. Strangelove* is an excellent black comedy. Briefly, American planes are ordered to bomb the Soviet Union by General Jack D. Ripper (Sterling Hayden), who is terrified of the pollution of his "precious bodily fluids" by Communist infiltration. Despite efforts to recall the wing by Peter Sellers—as President Mirkin Muffley—one plane, its radio crippled by a Russian attack, reaches and bombs its target, thus activating the Doomsday Bomb, Russian-built to act as a deterrent to nuclear warfare. This ultimate— and indefusable—weapon detonates all the atomic bombs in the world (to the tune of "We'll meet again, don't know where, don't know when"), sending all the film's magnificent caricatures to Kingdom Come.

The film is an exercise in perfection. There is not a visual, script, or directorial miscue in the entire production. Peter Sellers, who plays, in addition to President Muffley, Ripper's assistant group captain Lionel Mandrake and the ex-Nazi Doctor Strangelove, is brilliant; George C. Scott, as a rather stodgy gum-chewing general is superb; and the deadpan Hayden is perfect.

Then there's *The Tenth Victim,* a film of the future wherein a society channels violence into legalized murder-hunts. The film focuses on Ursula Andress' *Most Dangerous Game*–like search for Marcello Mastroianni. If nothing else, Andress is beautiful. The 1965 Italian film suffers, as have many before it, from poor dubbing.

In all fairness to *The Final War* (1962), it, like so many Japanese films, suffers from inferior dubbing. The plot is indecipherable, and the climactic blowup is less exciting visually than the most lax Godzilla free-for-all. Conversely, one interesting if minor effort is the unpretentious *Creation of the Humanoids* (1962), in which the main character becomes frustrated with man's perpetual reliance on robots and his relative loss of humanity. He— as well as the audience—is in for a shock, however, when our hero discovers that he is himself an R-36—the most advanced form of android, capable of reproducing . . . and, we soon discover, our direct ancestor. The film is a dandy, with interesting performances, sturdy direction, and a clever script. Even with its limited budget, it is much more than one might have expected it to be.

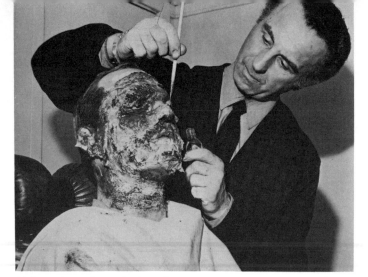

Make-up is applied to the face of a blast victim for Five Million Years to Earth.

Original poster art for Five Million Years to Earth, *the third film in the British Quatermass series.*

INVADERS FROM SPACE; VISITORS FROM SPACE

The third and final film to date in the British Dr. Quatermass series is the impressive *Five Million Years to Earth* (1967). The plot too often lapses into spurious profundity, making the film difficult to follow, but the basic premise is exciting. While excavating for a new subway system, workmen unearth a spaceship containing the remains of Martians. These Martians in silhouette look like man's pictures of the devil. The inference is that the image of Satan originated with these beings and was given substance throughout the ages by shadowy manifestations of the creatures above where their spaceship is buried.

Professor Quatermass eventually determines that the spaceship is cellularly "alive," having been powered by the thoughts of these creatures. The cell-structure of the ship "remembers" the long-dead Martians, and any human being who comes within range of the ship is overcome by the uncontrollable Martian telekinetic power. At the film's conclusion, this incredible telepathic might is accidentally released from the spaceship and runs rampant throughout London, all but destroying the city. Only when a scientist manages to ground the electrical impulses that have released the ship's energy is the menace halted.

The film is superbly photographed and has excellent special effects and performances by all concerned. It is a mature, provocative work.

More commercial and run-of-the-mill efforts range from *Navy vs. The Night Monsters* (1966), starring Mamie Van Doren and tentacled vegetables from space with acid for blood, to the entertaining *Day of the Triffids* (1962), based on the novel by John Wyndham. This production features plants that arrive on earth during a meteor shower that blinds everyone unfortunate enough to witness it.

Andrew Keir (with beard) and James Donald remove an ages-old alien corpse from a newly unburied spacecraft in Five Million Years to Earth.

With their death-dealing stinger vines, the ten-foot-tall Triffids begin to erase mankind entirely, with only a handful of Earthlings defending the blighted planet. Although it is soon found that fire can stop the creatures temporarily, it is discovered that sea water dissolves them into a chlorophyllic pulp. Needless to say, the sightless Earth is victorious. The film has good production values, adequate acting, and passable special effects. Animated Triffids by Harryhausen would have made the film a classic.

Invasion of the Star Creatures (1964) is a tongue-in-cheek parody of the genre in which two sexy women from space, along with their ten-foot-tall-carrot companions, come to Earth and are thwarted by a pair of inept soldiers. The film is funny in spots, ridiculous in others, but never boring. It's low-grade slapstick. *Santa Claus Conquers the Martians* (1964) is complete garbage, done "straight" for annual Christmas release. It's a gimmicky, trashy film that belongs in a class with *Hercules in New York* (1969). The Rankin-Bass *Rudolph the Red-Nosed Reindeer* (1965) and the Karloff *Grinch That Stole Christmas* (1970) are more what juvenile Christmas fantasy programming should be. And then there's one of the worst films ever made, *Frankenstein Meets the Space Monster* (1964), in which "Frankenstein" is nothing more than an android astronaut named Frank Reynolds who becomes disfigured when his spaceship is blasted from the sky by an about-to-invade-Earth-for-women spaceship. The disfigured robot stumbles from his wrecked spaceship and discovers the alien vehicle—which has now landed—eventually coming to battle the invaders' pet monster, Mull.

To show how utterly inane *Frankenstein Meets the Space Monster* really is: We are first introduced to Frank in an interview with newsmen. It would have been a press conference, but there wasn't a budget for more than three reporters.

167

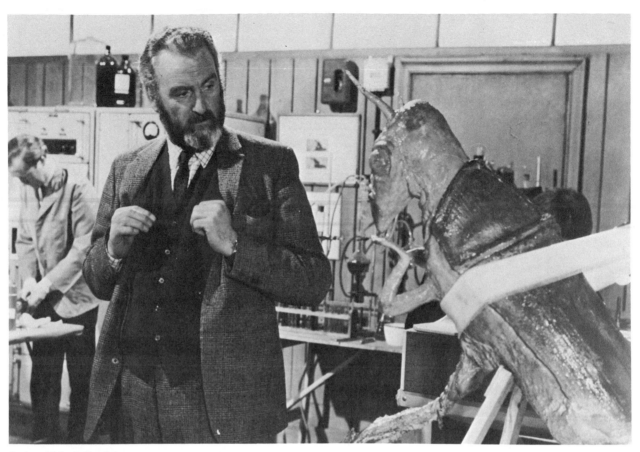

Andrew Keir studies the fossilized remains of his space creature in Five Million Years to Earth.

Howard Keel (right) stalks Triffids while they, in turn, stalk him. From Day of the Triffids.

"And now, gentlemen," Frank's creator announces, "I want to introduce you to the astronaut chosen for this mission . . . Frank Reynolds!"

Reynolds takes the podium and fields questions about his qualifications for the flight. He is finally asked why no one has ever heard of him before; the public does not know he's an android. Frank answers, "Well . . . I guess I'm just the shy type." Then he grins and freezes, his gears stuck. Looking like a plasticoated Howdy Doody, he just stares out at the newsmen wearing that ridiculous grimace. When asked what's wrong, he still stands there, just smiling.

The robot's creator calls a hasty end to the proceedings, explaining the freeze as tension, and brings Frank back to the lab. About to repair his creation, the doctor announces, "We have here, for all practical purposes, a normal man," at which point he rolls up the back of the skull and reveals a handful of gears and pulleys.

The good doctor gets it together, and Reynolds is off for Mars. The flight preparations and liftoff are all stock shots from an American Mercury launching, accompanied on the soundtrack by a rock score, the main song of which is something called "That's the Way It's Gotta Be."

Another disaster is *The Terrornauts* (1967), a low-budget, simple-minded film wherein half a dozen (British) Earthlings are spirited away to an uninhabited flying saucer. In due course, tapes left aboard the enormous craft tell them that this ship is all that remains of an ancient civilization wiped out by invading forces that are now en route to Earth. It seems the hostile aliens destroy all humanoid life forms; luckily, however, the tapes also tell how to use the saucer's arsenal, and the Earthlings turn these weapons against the approaching butchers and thoroughly annihilate them.

Everything about this film—from the acting to the sets to the script to the special effects—is terrible. But it's still better than *The Blood Beast from Outer Space* (1965), one Mr. Medra, who kidnaps Earth girls answering his advertisement in *Bikini Girl* magazine and sends them to Ganymede, one of the moons of Jupiter. This film was also released as both *The Night Caller* and *The Night Caller from Space*.

A particularly amusing science-fiction film—although the humor was unintentional—is *They Came from beyond Space* (1967), with Robert Hutton combatting invisible invaders. This one also stars Zia Mohyeddin and the usually distinguished Michael Gough and features beings from the moon who have come to Earth via meteorite. These creatures take over human beings with the condescending statement "The brains of these primitives seem quite suitable for our purposes"; and it's all down hill from there. The audience would have done well to echo the sentiments of one of the film's characters who asked, "What does a swarm of meteors have to do with me?" Yet even worse than this Amicus (makers of *Tales from the Crypt,* 1972, and *Vault of Horror,* 1973) disaster is *The Human Duplicators* (1964),

Bob Ball and Frankie Ray *welcome the alien visitors in* The Invasion of the Star Creatures.

an embarrassing effort. This one has George Nader stumble upon a plot hatched by Kolos, who arrives on Earth in an unintentionally transparent spaceship. Kolos, a giant of a man, is substituting androids for key personnel in science and government. Those who managed to stay awake until the end of the film were rewarded with Kolos' defeat through the efforts of a young blind girl.

Three Stooges in Orbit (1962) is, surprisingly, an entertaining film about Martian invaders who are thwarted by the dubious efforts of our heroes. Contrived, sometimes oversilly, and often just too much to swallow, the film is well directed, uses its small budget well, and is unpretentious fun.

An atmospheric and interesting effort from Japan that played many areas of the country on a double bill with *The Time Machine* is *Battle in Outer Space* (1960), a sturdy story of an invasion by aliens whose base is on the far side of the moon. After a bridge and a ship go flying through the air, Earth scientists decide that something is amiss. They trace the disturbances to the moon. The alien invaders are bested in space, after turning their antigravity ray loose on Earth, lifting men, buildings, and tanks. The film is more mature than the earlier Japanese effort *The Mysterians* (1959), and it hasn't one giant monster. Another Japanese film, *Warning from Space* (1968), is for kids only and features a good-guy emissary from space known as Star Man in a rehashing of the *Day the Earth Stood Still* theme.

Back in Europe, the British could have used Star Man when Earth was invaded by space robots in *Earth Dies Screaming* (1964), in which the invaders kill Earthlings and revive the corpses to do their dirty work. Earth is routed by Martians in *The Day Mars Invaded Earth* (1963). In this film, the Martians are composed of pure energy. *Invasion of the Animal People* (1963) is a good and sincere effort from Sweden with terrible added scenes filmed in the United States. In the original story, an enormous hairy being from space wreaks havoc among skiers in scenic snow-capped mountains. The film has a superlative mixing

170

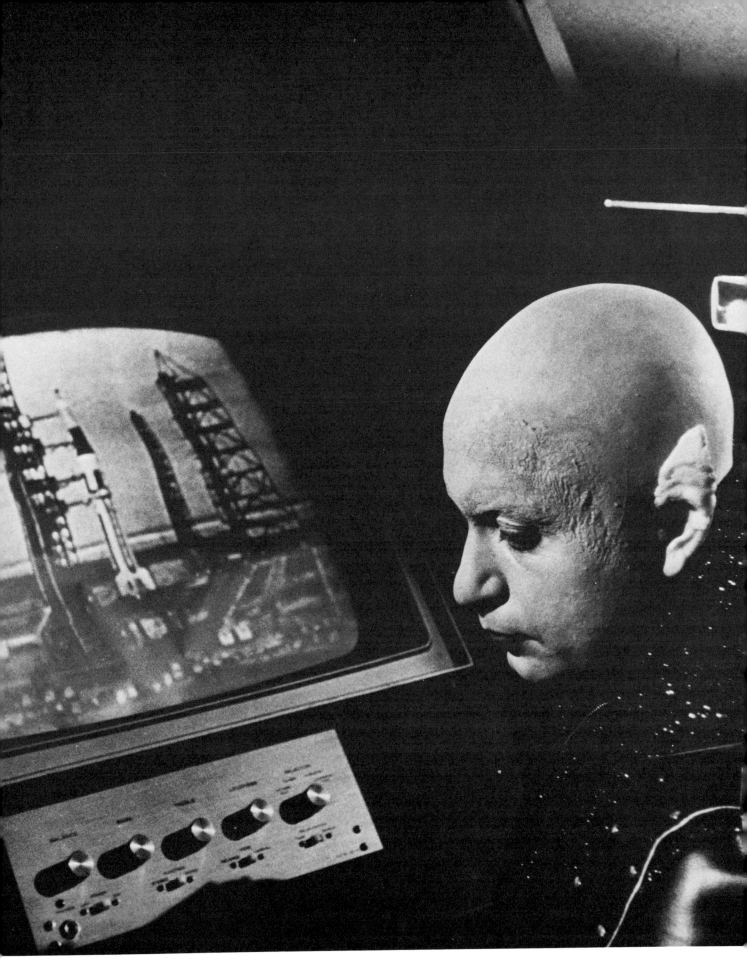

One of the poorly made-up
underlings of an invading alien
queen in Frankenstein Meets the
Space Monster.

Susan Hart is menaced by one of
The Slime People.

Jerry Lewis fails to impress his
other-worldly masters in Visit to a
Small Planet.

A slave of alien invaders. From
The Earth Dies Screaming.

of miniatures, monsters, and live actors, as well as excellent mood and a great deal of
suspense.

Unfortunately, as seen in the United States the film is an incredibly silly pastiche starring
John Carradine as a psychiatrist who tells this story as an example of why we must listen
to people who claim they've seen flying saucers. He opens his argument with this jumbled
assertion: "If we are unable to see the wood for the trees . . . if we fail to comprehend . . .

then there can be no hope for any type of control." As in the original release, the American version has the enormous Yeti-like creature as an escaped pet of visiting aliens.

A U.S. production is the low-budget but intriguing *Destination: Inner Space* (1966), starring Wende Wagner (of the *Green Hornet* TV series) and Gary Merrill (an escapee from the 1961 *Mysterious Island*) as underwater-research scientists who find a spaceship beneath the sea and retrieve a mysterious capsule from it. The following exchange between Doctor Lassiter (Merrill) and a naval officer stationed in the lab is typical.

COMMANDER WAYNE: Now listen, Doctor. You're a scientist. I understand your curiosity, but I don't understand your logic. This ship must have traveled through space millions of miles to get to this planet. We're dealing with something totally alien. That capsule might contain just instruments, or something simple like that. Or, it might contain something well beyond the realm of your understanding.

DOCTOR LASSITER: That's exactly the point, Commander. We're here to explore the unknown.

Needless to say, the scientist tampers with the capsule and from it comes a monster amphibian. After several encounters—in which the amphibian, like his 1951 cousin the Thing, cuts the sealab's electric and air supplies—the Earthlings win out. The film is extremely low-budgeted, has mediocre performances, but does create an aura of suspense. Though it is a composite of most every invader-from-space film, it provides ninety minutes of fast-paced entertainment.

Two particularly weak efforts were *Cyborg 2087* (1966), with Michael Rennie, and *The Cape Canaveral Monsters* (1960). In *Cyborg 2087,* Rennie—part man, part robot—journeys to the present to prevent the development of a scientific device that will make a future dictatorship possible. The irony of it all is that in the course of his errand of mercy, Rennie tinkers himself out of existence. *The Cape Canaveral Monsters* were not monsters, but people sent to Earth to sabotage our space program.

Planets Against Us (1960) is a run-of-the-mill invader film. Gore Vidal's *Visit to a Small Planet* features Jerry Lewis as a spaceman who visits Earth to research our strange customs. As is to be expected, he ends up marrying Joan Blackman. The idea of an alien visiting Earth to watch, rather than to invade, is a good one; for Jerry Lewis to portray that alien is a good idea in theory. Unfortunately, too much of the clown Lewis comes through. The man is capable of more subtle comedy than, after taking a thrashing, announcing of his arm, "It don't hit, it don't hit!" or levitating his car from the thruway to avoid traffic. However, Lewis carries some lines better than most anyone else could, such as the one wherein he asks for the girl's hand in marriage, explaining to her doubting father that he's saved up enough "glubdingles" to make her happy and comfortable. The film also stars science-fiction-film veteran Earl Holliman (the cook in *Forbidden Planet* and a doomed scientist in *The Power*).

173

One of these people is a super-mind from the far future! Earl Holliman (back to us), Nehemiah Persoff, Michael Rennie, Richard Carlson, Arthur O'Connell, George Hamilton, and Suzanne Pleshette watch as a paper skewered on a pencil whirls of its own volition, controlled by the alien. From The Power.

THE MIND, AND MAN THE INVADER

A telepath, Adam Hart (Michael Rennie), is the featured character in George Pal's film *The Power* (1967). With motives never made perfectly clear, Hart has been killing people and subsequently erasing the memory of their existence from the minds of the living. Hart becomes aware of the existence of a telepath with powers equal to his own. This supermind, unaware of his own inherent powers, is one of the members of a small scientific team. To pinpoint this other telepath, Hart methodically kills all the members of the research unit. Only George Hamilton does not succumb to Hart's mental assaults. Hamilton is exposed to the strange and ethereal powers of the diabolical Hart, first finding that records of his past have been destroyed, then gradually losing all touch with reality, and finally surviving an all-out mental shellacking before his own abilities induce, in Hart, a heart-attack.

Abetted by an inventive Miklos Rosza score (unlike anything ever created by the composer of the *Ben-Hur* and *El Cid* scores), superlative special effects, and a lively pace, the film is an enthralling, constantly surprising science-fiction classic. The photography constantly underlines the mood of the film, one of hovering death in which the very foundations of the characters' minds are mere putty in the face of the awesome invader. The characters are forced to hallucinate terrible nightmares—such as the disappearance of doors and windows from their offices—and the haunting of their waking hours by real nightmares. Hamilton, at a carnival, finds himself attacked by the toys and amusements; he mounts a merry-go-round and wakes to find himself being whirled to death in a centrifuge at the space center. The film is a mature, terrifying production that deserved much better distribution than it received.

Another excellent film in which a man gets carried away with his own power is *Man with the X-Ray Eyes* (1963), in which Ray Milland ingests a chemical mixture that enables him to see through solid objects. Eventually his vision gets out of hand. Milland keeps seeing

George Hamilton finds himself on
a nightmare merry-go-round in a
dream sequence from The
Power.

Unable to see the real world, Ray Milland drives his car off the road. From The Man with the X-Ray Eyes.

Don Rickles, as a carny boss, chides Ray Milland, The Man with the X-Ray Eyes.

The Nautilus ferries beneath the waves. From Capt. Nemo and the Underwater City.

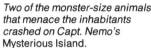
Two of the monster-size animals that menace the inhabitants crashed on Capt. Nemo's Mysterious Island.

deeper and deeper into the reality of the tangible world until, at the film's conclusion, his mind unable to cope with that which he sees, he stumbles upon a revival meeting where the congregation is chanting, "If thine eye offend thee, pluck it out"—which he does.

The film is convincing, if a bit contrived and moralistic as it creeps toward its inevitable conclusion. The acting, sets, and special effects are good. Unfortunately, the film too often bogs down in the trite. But Milland's progressive insanity, his lowering himself to becoming a freak in a circus sideshow, and his inability to cope with the new and terrifying visions that assault his mind are handled with intelligence and convey great impact.

Not particularly impressive is a Japanese picture, *The H-Man* (1959), a minor effort that doubled with *The Woman Eater* (1959) in many parts of the country. The H-Man—or, more accurately, *men*—have been changed from people to amorphous green blobs by radiation. These blobs thrive on people—whom they eat and disintegrate in a matter of seconds—until destroyed by flame-throwing policemen. The technical aspects of the film are barely passable. But even *The H-Man* was better than *The Crawling Hand* (1963), a

Atlantis, the Lost Continent,
before and after it became lost.

The original ad art for Capt. Nemo and the Underwater City. *Pictured are Chuck Connors (left) and Robert Ryan.*

Herbert Lom's interpretation of Capt. Nemo from Mysterious Island.

Peter Cushing unveils lovely Susan Denberg, the "monster" in Frankenstein Created Woman.

The British ad art for Frankenstein Created Woman.

poignant tale of a college student who falls under the influence of a dead astronaut's disembodied hand. Then there was *The Electronic Monster* (1960), featuring the use of human beings as guinea pigs in weird scientific experiments.

Village of the Giants (1965) is a Bert I. Gordon ruination of the H. G. Wells classic *Food of the Gods,* turned to a rock 'n' teen effort with only fair special effects. Coming after Gordon's excellent *Magic Sword* (1962), this film was a disappointment.

Curse of the Fly (1965) continued the Fly saga in name alone—this awful black-and-white effort does the series no credit. Besides, any film that opens with a mutated girl running through the forest in her underwear in slow motion just *can't* be good. The girl was one of the mutants produced by experimentation with the matter transmitter, and only when the mutants escape and lace into the scientists does the film pick up. But it's too little too late.

Superscience was the cornerstone of George Pal's fanciful *Atlantis, the Lost Continent,* a 1961 release featuring, among other things, filmed-but-never-used footage of the burning of Rome from *Quo Vadis* (1951). Pal used it to augment the sinking of his Atlantean paradise. Walt Disney, who had given us such fine science-fiction fantasies as *The Shaggy Dog* (1959) and *Twenty Thousand Leagues under the Sea* (1954), started wading through live-action trivia with such efforts as *The Absent-minded Professor* (1960), *Son of Flubber* (1962), and *The Misadventures of Merlin Jones* (1963). These films were not entirely without merit—there were some clever technical effects and acceptable acting in the flubber films by Fred MacMurray—but these efforts were far below Disney's abilities, as *Mary Poppins* would illustrate in 1967. Yet, lukewarm as these films were, they appear brilliant when compared with Disney's films of the seventies.

181

With *Seventh Voyage of Sinbad* (1958) and *Three Worlds of Gulliver* (1960) behind him, Ray Harryhausen stuck to the classics, animating monster crabs, birds, and bees for *Mysterious Island* in 1961. Excellent special effects notwithstanding (the sequence wherein the monster bee attacks two of the party is incredible), *Mysterious Island* is distinguished by the presence of Herbert Lom as Captain Nemo. His brooding cynicism fits the role like a glove.

Some old standards had another go at it when Frankenstein and Hammer again joined forces (with Peter Cushing once more in the fore as the mad doctor) in *The Evil of Frankenstein* (1964), a quality Frankenstein film that brought us a monster closer, in face and carriage, to the Karloff portrayal than Hammer's previous efforts. And the fiery climax is superb! There were also *Frankenstein Created Woman* (1969) and *Frankenstein Must Be Destroyed* (1970), but these were nothing more than sex-and-blood entries, certainly not worthy of Hammer.

Die Monster Die (1965) brought back Boris Karloff as a monster who, as in *The Invisible Ray,* was infected by radiation from space and was transformed into a grotesque monster. And Jerry Lewis turned in his best directorial/starring effort ever in the sensitive, funny, clever, sincere story of a weak, buck-toothed college professor who quaffs a potion and becomes "Joe Cool" on the College Campus in *The Nutty Professor* (1963), a modified retelling of the Jekyll-Hyde tale. Lewis can be a resourceful filmmaker when he wants to be, and this production proves it.

One of the more frightening visions of the mind and soul of man gone awry came from John Wyndham's novel *The Midwich Cuckoos,* directed by Wolf Rilla as *Village of the Damned* (1960). For several hours, the people of a small English town become unconscious under the influence of a mysterious force, and it is discovered soon after the occurence that all women capable of bearing children are pregnant. Their offspring are children who, before reaching their teens, can control peoples' minds. Also, there is a strange camaraderie among the children, who exhibit a marked taste for world subjugation. The youngsters are finally destroyed when one of the men in the town grabs a case of dynamite and blows himself and the children sky high. The children are wholly convincing in their cold, ethereal manner, and the blond-haired, glowing-eyed offspring are a devilish, unnerving lot.

In a sequel, *Children of the Damned* (1964), six different children are discovered at various points throughout the world and brought to London for study by two UNESCO investigators. The film loses its way when one of the pair uses the children's powers for his own personal vendetta, and the youngsters are subsequently destroyed by army artillery while hiding in a church. The film, despite draggy moments, is a good one, handled with skill and maturity.

Barbara Ferris and the Midwich
Cuckoos known as the Children
of the Damned.

George Sanders and Barbara
Shelley cower from their
telekinetic son in Village of the
Damned, based on John
Wyndham's novel The Midwich
Cuckoos.

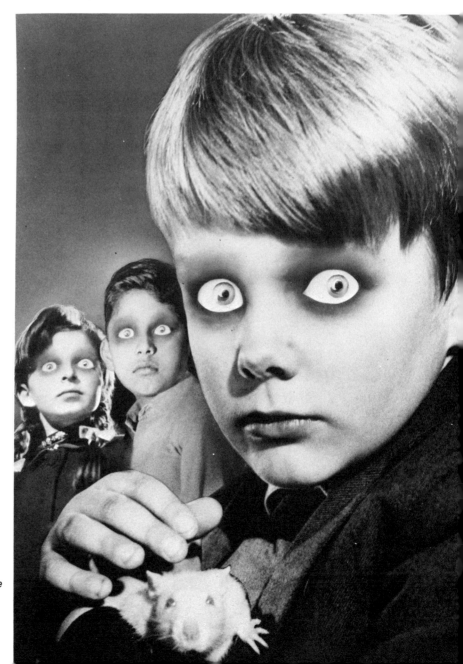

Their eyes ablaze with
destructive force, the Children of
the Damned prepare to subjugate
their cruel adult masters.

The Seventies

Kim Hunter, as Zira, holds up a protest banner in Beneath the Planet of the Apes.

A gathering of gorillas voice their support for militaristic action proposed by General Ursus. From Beneath the Planet of the Apes.

184

Science fiction in the seventies has been all but dominated by apes. Four sequels to *Planet of the Apes* have been released, and despite declarations to the contrary, there is no end in sight.

A strength of the original *Planet of the Apes* was the novelty of it all—the concept, the sets, and the apes were unique, and this uniqueness was responsible for much of the original film's appeal. The sequels were without this newness of premise. They had to rely more on characterization, action, and plot. And in every film—although the actual quality of the productions dropped radically—the plots became more clever and more intriguing.

Let us look at the series as a whole. Two different spaceflights break the time barrier and land on Earth in the fortieth century. It is a world dominated by apes, who lord it over the humans, who cannot speak or communicate. The apes, on the other hand, can read, write . . . and perform brain surgery (*Planet of the Apes*, 1968).

After a severe famine, the apes launch an expedition into the Forbidden Zone to secure land and discover what legendary evil lurks therein. Meanwhile, the two survivors of each spaceflight—independently of one another—have gone to the Fobidden Zone and been taken prisoner by mutants, living in the underground remains of New York City, who worship the alpha-omega bomb, the most deadly of all atomic weapons. The apes invade the mutant catacombs and kill the occupants, and one of the astronauts detonates the bomb (*Beneath the Planet of the Apes*, 1970).

All life on Earth has been destroyed. Just before the explosion, however, three apes—two male and one female—escaped to 1973 in one of the two abandoned spaceships. They land in Southern California and are eventually shot to death (*Escape from the Planet of the Apes,* 1971).

However, the female ape has given birth, and the baby is found and raised by the owner of a circus. In the 1990s, a space plague kills all Earth's cats and dogs, and apes are domesticated and are kept as pets. When it is discovered that they make good waiters, janitors, and workers, they are trained. Meanwhile, matured to "manhood," the ape from the future—who can speak and think, having inherited his parents' abilities—leads the enslaved apes in revolt and subjugates the humans (*Conquest of the Planet of the Apes,* 1972). War for possession of the Earth is waged among the various kinds of apes—gorillas, orangutans, chimpanzees—the humans, and the mutants (scarred by atomic warfare resulting from the ape revolt). After all of the wars, everyone vows to try to live in peace (*Battle for the Planet of the Apes,* 1973).

Running full circle, it is obvious that by the fortieth century, the humans have fallen to utter ruin. The use of the classic vicious circle in the Apes series is fantastic. The idea that had the astronauts not gone to the future, the apes could not have escaped into the past, their son would not have fostered a revolt of the apes, and there would have been no Planet of the Apes to which the astronauts could go, is tantalizing food for thought.

James Franciscus and Linda
Harrison (as Nova) plan a course
of action in Beneath the Planet of
the Apes.

Brent and Cornelius (David
Watson) dispute a point in
Beneath the Planet of the Apes.

James Gregory (left) and Maurice Evans (right) heed the words of a wise man regarding their proposed expedition into the Forbidden Zone.

James Franciscus is lead by mutants into what used to be Grand Central Station. From Beneath the Planet of the Apes.

The series could conceivably go on forever, since the fate of the other of the two rockets is unknown. Apes could have utilized the ship to visit another planet and may return to repopulate the earth after the alpha-omega radiation has dissipated. It might then work out that the apes evolve into human beings and that Heston, in *Planet of the Apes,* actually came from the far future and landed in the past. . . .

In any event, with the exception of *Planet of the Apes,* the films are simple, digestible science fiction. They do not ram any grandiose philosophies down the viewers' throats; rather, they present smatterings of moral thought undisguised by allegory.

Satire plays an important part in the films. The following from the Mass of the Holy Bomb, practiced by the mutants in *Beneath the Planet of the Apes,* is a clever piece of writing and a frightening bit of satire.

The heavens declare the glory of the Bomb, and the firmament showeth His handiwork. He descendeth from the outermost part of Heaven, and there is nothing hid from the heat thereof. There is neither speech nor language; yet His voice is heard among them. Glory be to the Bomb and to the Holy Fallout, as it was in the beginning, is now, and ever shall be, world without end. O Mighty and everlasting Bomb, who came down among us to make Heaven into Earth, lighten our darkness, O instrument of God . . . grant us thy peace. Amen.

Beneath the Planet of the Apes also contains two interesting discourses on man and human nature. The first is read from the apes' Sacred Scrolls to Heston as he is about to embark on a journey into the Forbidden Zone to discover the riddle of the Planet of the Apes.

Beware the beast man, for he is the devil's pawn. Alone among God's primates, he kills for sport . . . or lust . . . or greed. Yea, he will murder his brother to possess his brother's land. Let him not breed in great numbers, for he will make a desert of his home . . . and yours. Shun him . . . for he is the harbinger of death.

And General Ursus, commander of the gorilla army, delivers the following morale booster to his men:

Members of the citizens' council, I am a simple soldier, and as a soldier, I see things simply. I don't say all humans are evil simply because their skin is white; no! But our Great Lawgiver tells us that never, *never* will the human have the ape's divine faculty for being able to distinguish between evil and good. The only good human is a dead human!

On a more brutal, less fantastic note, is Stanley Kubrick's highly controversial *A Clockwork Orange* (1971). The dominant philosophy of the film can be neatly capsulized in the following line, wherein a priest discusses the Ludivico treatment—a treatment that makes one sick when thoughts of violence enter his mind—with protagonist Alex: "The question is whether or not this technique really makes a man good. Goodness comes from within. Goodness is chosen. When a man cannot choose, he ceases to be a man."

Alex is a member of a gang of hoodlums who roam about raping, murdering, and mugging

Roddy McDowall, Kim Hunter, and Sal Mineo arrive in 1973 after they escape in Escape from the Planet of the Apes.

Ursula Andress as she appears in The Tenth Victim.

some time in the near future. Alex is captured and sent to jail; he is given the Ludivico treatment and returned to the world of the law abiding. The ensuing situations are eloquent and highly stylized, with great impact. Technically, the film is flawless. The lighting, editing, photography, and art direction are expert. The battle sequences—between Alex's gang and a rival gang and between Alex and two of his companions—are choreographed to Rossini's *The Thieving Magpie* Overture. They are among the most bizarre ballets ever filmed.[14] The film is faithful in both theme and plot to the Anthony Burgess novel of the same name. It is not science fiction in the same gadget-laden sense as was *2001: A Space Odyssey,* but it is an arresting, rattling view of the near future.

After *Planet of the Apes,* Charlton Heston did a minor film about football called *Number One* (1970). Following that came his second science fiction film and the second inadequate filming of Richard Matheson's brilliant novel *I Am Legend.* Filmed first in 1964 as *The Last Man on Earth,* with Vincent Price, *I Am Legend* now became *The Omega Man* (1971), a tale of the last "normal" human being on Earth. Everyone else has been mutated by germ warfare to white-skinned creatures that come out only at night—vampires, for easy reference, although they do not suck blood. Heston portrays a scientist who was experimenting to find a cure for the coming plague; the antidote was untried when war broke out, but Heston injected himself with it. There is a truly terrifying aura about the goings-on for the first half of the film, during which Heston battles the vampires with a rifle, fire, and his bare hands. Only when Heston is captured does the film go downhill.

About to be killed by Anthony Zerbe[15]—who uses Heston's demise to signify the end of one era and the beginning of another—Heston manages to escape. Waiting for him is a lovely black woman with a motorcycle. Heston and his attractive savior mount the bike, and he pilots the vehicle over car tops, up stairs, and away from danger. The woman directs Heston to a small commune where a group of people succumbing very slowly to the plague have set up residence.

One of the incredible sets from the James Bond epic You Only Live Twice.

Charlton Heston tries to persuade the vampirized Rosalind Cash to abandon her ways in The Omega Man.

Charlton Heston is trapped by vampires in his fortress residence. From The Omega Man.

Naturally, Heston falls in love with the woman, providing racial commentary, but by the end of the film she has become a vampire. Heston saves her from Zerbe, dying in the process, and the sole male adult member of the village takes her under his wing. He also takes a bottle of Heston's blood, which serves as an antidote to the plague.

The "salvation" of the innocent as Heston's blood "cleanses" the earth, his mock crucifixion—he is skewered against a pole by a spear, his arms flung perpendicular to his body—and, of course, the fact that Heston has played most every biblical hero with the exception of Christ all lead one to the obvious point of the film. But don't be misled. Heston explained, "The Christ reference was not meant to be taken as seriously as most people took it."

After a vacation from science fiction in which he got *Skyjacked* (1972), Heston returned as Frank Thorne, a New York City policeman of the year 1999, in *Soylent Green* (1973). This film is better by far than *The Omega Man*. Based on a Harry Harrison novel, *Make Room, Make Room,* the movie follows Heston's investigation into the production of an artificial wafer known as soylent green, ostensibly made from algae. It is the main staple of New York's forty million people, since meat, vegetables, and all natural sustenance have long been unobtainable.

During the film, Heston beats up several persons, makes love to Leigh Taylor-Young, and has some beautiful and sensitive conversations with the late Edward G. Robinson (in his last film role, as Sol Cohen, detective Heston's aged roommate). The high point of the film shows Robinson, tired of the stuffy, inhumane life in this Brave New World, in an auditorium where visitors are put to death to the tune of their favorite musical piece and Cinerama-sized movies of the world that once was.

Robinson has come here to die, but before his time is up, Heston comes to him. Through a glass partition, he talks with the dying man. Heston's reaction to what is appearing on the screen—images of a nature and world he had never known existed—is overwhelming. His awe at this vision of flowers and lakes, mountains and trees is absolute; when Robinson asks Heston if he can now understand the old man's bitterness at the congested turn society has taken, Heston can only mumble, in reverent humility, "How could I have known . . . how could I have known?"

By the end of the film, Heston makes his way to a soylent plant and discovers that human bodies, not algae, are what's being broken down and transformed into soylent green—for the seas have died long ago. Fighting vast odds and getting shot, stabbed, and bludgeoned, Heston finally gets his message to the world: "Soylent green is people! "

The film is effective when it deals with confrontations between well-rounded, established personalities—Heston and Robinson, Heston and his police boss, Heston and Chuck Connors (a soylent agent). It is at its worst when Heston meets a woman kept in an apartment house for the sole purpose of entertaining its occupant. He falls in love with the woman, who, because she is a "piece of furniture," cannot love him.

The seventies have produced only two major science-fiction disasters, *Gas-s-s* (1970) and *The Crazies* (1973). *Gas-s-s* is a Roger Corman satire in which a deadly gas escapes into the air from a defense plant. The gas speeds up the aging process and pushes everyone over the age of twenty-five into old age and death. In a contrived and silly story, all the people under the deadly age spend their time looking for an identity, trying to find themselves, knowing that death is imminent.

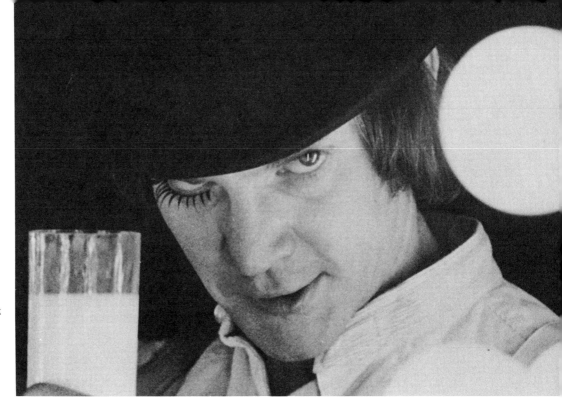

Malcolm McDowell as Alex in
Stanley Kubrick's A Clockwork
Orange.

The Crazies, from George Romero, director of the now-classic Night of the
Living Dead (1968), is a cheap story of the accidental spilling of biological-war material
into the water supply of a small New England town.

Conversely, The Andromeda Strain (1971) is one of the great science-fiction films.
Director Robert Wise didn't miss a trick. His actors (James Olson, Arthur Hill, and David
Wayne) are not superstars, but they are solid performers all. His sets are superb and
thoroughly convincing, his photography is striking, and the story, based on the bestseller
by Michael Crichton, is gripping, intelligent, and frightening.

The story centers around a bacterium nicknamed Andromeda, brought back from space
by an American satellite. The space probe lands in a small Western town and is opened
by the local physician. All the townspeople are killed, with the exception of a drunk and a
baby. It is they who eventually provide the clue to the antidote for the Andromeda plague
(utter lack or excess of oxygen in the blood).

Four scientists are called to an underground complex to see what caused the deaths.
Sequences of two scientists rummaging through the contaminated town in protective
radiation suits are fantastic—corpses litter the streets, their blood turned to powder by
Andromeda. Another scene of horrifying impact is one wherein a jet pilot, flying
reconnaissance over the deadly town, finds every plastic component of his plane turning
to powder, followed by the disintegration of his own skin and blood. The interrelationship
among the scientists is tense, real, and engrossing, and the inclusion of a grumpy,
middle-aged woman (Kate Reid) as part of the group was a stroke of genius. Her
emotional reactions to situations provide contrast to the sterile, laboratory-like reactions
of her male counterparts.

The great Godzilla as he appears in his latest epic, Godzilla vs. the Smog Monster.

Michael Sacks and Valerie Perrine on the planet Trafalmagor in Slaughterhouse-Five.

Earth II (1971) is a modest and mildly entertaining film about a space station that has to prevent the Earth's being blown apart by an escaped missile. It's typical run-of-the-mill material with excellent special effects but barely pedestrian performances.

Silent Running, on the other hand, makes a wholly noble effort to overcome a small budget and make an impressive show of itself. It only partially succeeds. Directed by Douglas Trumbull, the special-effects man responsible for much of the technical majesty of *2001: A Space Odyssey, Silent Running* handles its actors and effects well but is weak and unconvincing with its plot and theme. In the story, the last floral-life forms from Earth are kept alive on a giant spaceship manned by several astronauts and their little robot helpers known as Drones.

When the order is given from Earth to destroy the greenhouses and return home, star Bruce Dern is crushed. This is the end of nature, in his eyes. So instead of sacrificing the plants, Dern kills the other members of the party and, pushing the ship out of Earth orbit (to the tune of an awful vocal soundtrack by Joan Baez), saunters about the solar system before going mad from loneliness. Then, placing the Drones in charge of the greenhouse, he destroys himself. Bruce Dern's performance is magnificent. He does a superlative job with a difficult role as the space-age Johnny Appleseed. The Drones are convincingly mobile—manned by amputees—and the models of the ships are well appointed. Still, the film features an obligatory sequence of psychedelic space tripping, akin to Kubrick's journey through the time-space vortex in *2001: A Space Odyssey,* and sports Kubrick-like close-ups of the planets, huge spaceships, and so forth. A comparison between Kubrick's fourteen-million-dollar epic and Trumbull's one-million-dollar effort is inevitable. In such a race, *Silent Running* is left light-years behind.

THX-1138 (1971) is a fine film directed by George Lucas, whose 1973 *American Graffiti* was a smash hit, both critically and at the box office. This is another variation on the 1984 theme in which a man known as THX rebels against a robotized, sterile society. Lucas transposed the world of the future very effectively from an original screenplay by himself and Walter Murch. The gleaming, silver faces of the robot police and the white clothing of the human beings give forceful emphasis to the society's tragic "cleanliness," emphasizing that this is a world in which love, emotion, and happiness are unlawful. Unfortunately, the world of the twenty-fifth century did not appeal to theatergoers— primarily because of abysmal distribution—and this feature did not do at all well.[16]

Another box-office failure—and this one, rightfully so—was *ZPG* (1972) (the initials stand for Zero Population Growth), an absurd story of a future wherein birth has been outlawed. Oliver Reed does an admirable job with his role as Geraldine Chaplin's husband, but the film is self-conscious and tends to preach. That is not a sin, but it is bad filmmaking when the picture simultaneously puts its audience to sleep.

Then there's *Slaughterhouse-Five* (1972), technically and aesthetically a fine adaptation of the Kurt Vonnegut "time-tripping" book. Billy Pilgrim, as he explains it, has become "unstuck in time" and journeys from period to period in his own life. As a film, *Slaughterhouse-Five* is fine; however, one must appreciate Vonnegut's humor and sense of justice to enjoy the picture.

Another film that suffered an unjust fate at the box office was *Forbin Project* (1970), which, while still in release, received a title change and became *Colossus,* returning to the original name of the novel on which it was based. As it was, the title change helped not at all. *Colossus: The Forbin Project* (a third and final label) is the story of a computer gone mad. Colossus is the ultimate computer and is therefore not content to serve humans. The man-made monster contacts its Soviet counterpart, and the two plot to enslave the world.

Robots of a less ambitious nature are the featured stars of *Westworld* (1973), director Michael Crichton's look at a Disneyland for adults. Westworld is a reconstruction of different period settings wherein the clientele—for a formidable price—can live out their fantasies as gunfighters, charioteers, and whatever. The historical mockups are peopled with androids programmed to make the human visitor look good at whatever he tries, be that gunfighting, fisticuffs, or any other form of competition. All goes well until robot Yul Brynner decides he's sick of losing and goes on the warpath.

The film is meticulous—a trait of Michael Crichton, author of *The Andromeda Strain* and *The Terminal Man*—but emerges a laboratory-sterile chiller desperately in need of the humanity a Robert Wise or a Jack Arnold could have supplied.

To date, the seventies have given us but four monster-on-the-loose epics: *Yog* (1971), another of those interminable and juvenile Japanese monster films; *Godzilla vs. the Smog Monster* (1972), wherein the immortal Godzilla battles Hedorah, a flying creature that

*Bruce Dern operates on his
robotic aide, one of the
mechanical drones, in a scene
from* Silent Running.

thrives on all forms of pollution; *Night of the Lepus* (1972), about giant rabbits; and *Son of Blob* (1972), a tongue-in-cheek revival of the old slime monster. This one contains such witty touches as Godfrey Cambridge getting up from his easy chair to adjust the TV set, returning to his seat without seeing the Blob sitting there . . . and being devoured. The monster is finally trapped in an ice-skating rink and frozen . . . just like his old man.

Two other returnees to celluloid life were Frankenstein and his monster. Two new Frankenstein films came to us from Great Britain—*Horror of Frankenstein* (1970), an engrossing but sadistic retelling of the original tale, and *Frankenstein vs. the Monster from Hell* (1973).

Of course, the most interesting and offbeat revival of the seventies is *Flesh Gordon* (1972). With a million-dollar budget, this X-rated science-fiction spoof has good production values and impressive sets, costumes, and special effects. The acting—or rather, performing—is what one might expect from a film wherein the hero lands on the planet Porno and does battle with Jim Danforth's animated penisaurus. (Now we've only to wait and see what they'll call the X-rated update of Buck Rogers. . . .)

196

Science Fiction on Television

Adam West as TV's Batman.

The snappy Batmobile

Burt Ward as Robin in the TV series Batman.

Science fiction on television has had a long and diversified life. Early, rather unsophisticated space series, such as *Captain Video* (1949), starring Al Hodge as the interplanetary traveler; *Tom Corbett, Space Cadet* (1950), starring Frankie Thomas as a space-suited star hopper; and *Superman* (1950), starring George Reeves as the Kryptonian man of steel, established a fun, fantasy-filled format for TV science fiction that would serve as a model for children's imagi-realm programming for years to come. Indeed, the fact that *Superman* is still a major staple of the rerun circuit seems indicative

Richard Basehart (left), David Hedison, and the crew of the Seaview in Irwin Allen's TV series Voyage to the Bottom of the Sea.

A UFO from the TV show of the same name.

of the success of the light, fanciful formula. And doubtless, had *Tom Corbett* and *Captain Video* not been somewhat emasculated by advances in technology, they, too, would be alive and well today.

ABC brought the fantasy world of Walt Disney to home screens in 1954 and, as of 1974, the metamorphosed *Disneyland–Walt Disney Presents–Walt Disney's Wonderful World of Color* is still going strong. During its long run, such adventure heroes as Zorro, Texas John Slaughter, and Swamp Fox and cartoon characters such as Ludwig von Drake have been welcome guests in living rooms the world over.

The mature and often stimulating *Science Fiction Theatre* came to us in 1955, and during its brief run, host Truman Bradley took us through many not-so-impossible worlds of science fiction. Many episodes were merely extensions of existing knowledge or studies in the mind, space research, and such. One particularly striking segment had, for example, a man in a movie theater mesmerized by the flickering screen image to duplicate a murder being enacted in the film. The casual attitude with which the man commits the crime—and the subsequent study of this man by cold, logical scientists mindless of the victim—seems to foreshadow a world of sterile scientific orientation.

Zacherly and Vampira were horror–science-fiction film-show hosts who had their respective East and West Coast debut in 1955. Zacherly would often interrupt films featured on his *Shock Theatre* and interject tongue-in-cheek bits of action that fit the flow of the film. Alfred Hitchcock, who also arrived in a 1955 teleseries, had more "respect" for

Angela Cartwright, as Penny Robinson, and Lou Wagner in The Haunted Lighthouse *episode of* Lost in Space. *Wagner played an alien named J-5.*

Jonathan Harris as Dr. Smith, with robot friend from Irwin Allen's hit TV series Lost in Space.

Michael Rennie as the Keeper in The Keeper *episode of* Lost in Space.

Jonathan Harris (left), Mark Goddard (as Don West) and Michael Conrad (as Creech) in the Fugitives in Space *episode of* Lost in Space.

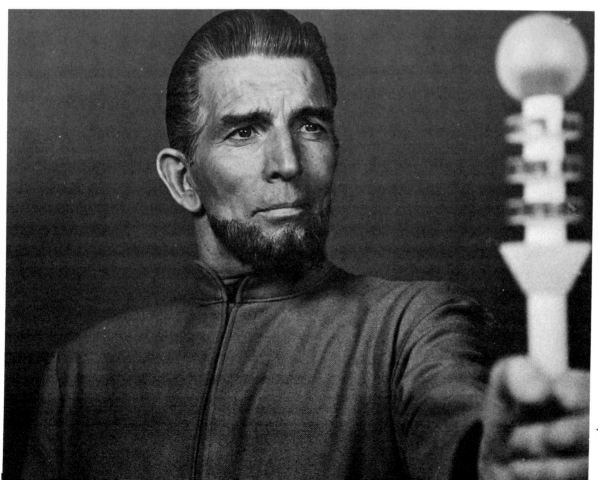

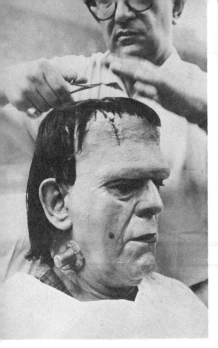

Boris Karloff is made up, for the last time, as the Frankenstein Monster for the Lizard's Leg, Owlet's Wing *episode of* Route 66.

Ray Walston (left) and Bill Bixby in the My Favorite Martian *TV* show.

Robert Vaughn and David McCallum in the MGM teleseries Man from U.N.C.L.E.

his work, although he was not averse to introducing or concluding a suspense drama with some cynical or snidely witty remark about it.

The British series *The Invisible Man* premiered in 1958, and a special investigator six inches tall, carried about in a briefcase, was the substance of 1959's *World of Giants*.

That same year, Rod Serling's *Twilight Zone* began a long and prosperous life on the tube. The finest fantasy-scripting talent in the world, men such as Serling, the late Charles Beaumont, and Richard Matheson, among others, contributed their skills to the series. During its historic run *Twilight Zone* brought such talented actors as William Shatner (in "Nightmare at 20,000 Feet," the story of a man who sees a gremlin crawling on the wing outside his plane window), Buster Keaton, Lee Marvin, Roddy McDowall, Ross Martin, Ed Wynn, Inger Stevens, Cliff Robertson, and Burgess Meredith to home screens in

Frankie Thomas in 1952 as Tom Corbett, Space Cadet *for ABC TV.*

Richard Deacon is a factory owner who is replaced by a machine (Robby the Robot's third screen appearance) in The Brain Center at Whipples *episode of* Twilight Zone.

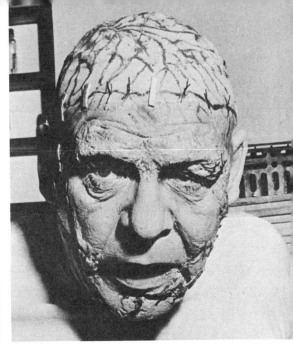

Buster Keaton (right) and Stanley Adams in the Once Upon a Time segment of Twilight Zone.

Tracy Stafford becomes lost in the fourth dimension in the Twilight Zone episode entitled Little Girl Lost.

Lon Chaney, Jr. as the Frankenstein Monster in the Tales of Tomorrow TV series.

perpetually high-quality shows of science fiction and fantasy. Serling's *Night Gallery* series (1971), with the emphasis on horror, seldom had the quality of *Twilight Zone,* despite guest appearances by Leonard Nimoy, Richard Kiley, Joan Crawford, Roddy McDowall, Vincent Price, Yaphet Kotto, and Edward G. Robinson.

Mr. Ed (1961) gave Alan Young (of George Pal's *Time Machine*) a successful series, and *Man from U.N.C.L.E.* and *My Living Doll* (both 1964, with Robert Vaughn and Julie Newmar, respectively) gave viewers more sophisticated serial-like thrills and eye-filling spectacle . . . respectively.

My Favorite Martian (1963), with Ray Walston and Bill Bixby; *Bewitched* (1964), with Elizabeth Montgomery and Agnes Moorhead; *The Addams Family* (1964), with Carolyn Jones and John Astin; *The Munsters* (1964), with Yvonne DeCarlo and Fred Gwynne; *My*

The stars of The Zanti Misfits episode of The Outer Limits. The misfits are Zanti prisoners sent to Earth instead of being jailed or killed on their home planet.

201

David McCallum portrays a man thrown eons ahead in the evolutionary scale in The Sixth Finger *episode of* Outer Limits.

Mother the Car (1965), with Jerry Van Dyke; *I Dream of Jeannie* (1965), with Larry Hagman and Barbara Eden; *Get Smart* (1965), more spy thrills with Don Adams and Ed Platt; Great Britain's *Secret Agent* (1965), with Patrick McGoohan; *Batman* (1966), with Adam West and Burt Ward; *Green Hornet* (1967), with Van Williams and the late Bruce Lee; *Mission: Impossible* (1966), with Peter Graves; and the British *Avengers* (1966), with Diana Rigg and Patrick Macnee were varied, not-always-successful embellishments on old spy, witch, fantasy, or serial themes.

Additions to the time-travel genre included Irwin Allen's *Time Tunnel* and the CBS folly *It's About Time,* with Frank Aletter (husband of *Time Tunnel*'s Lee Meriwether), Imogene Coca, and Joe E. Ross. Coca and Ross were cavepeople; as the theme music explains it, "It's about time, it's about space. It's about two men in the strangest place. It's about time.

It's about flight. Traveling faster than the speed of light. It's about two astronauts. It's about their fate. It's about a woman and her prehistoric mate." Both time-travel shows featured reams of stock footage from feature films. *It's About Time* borrowed half of its first episode from *Beast of Hollow Mountain,* and *Time Tunnel* every week plopped two souls lost in time into various periods of history . . . but only those periods from which stock footage could be lifted (*Khartoum, The Alamo,* etc.).

Star Trek with William Shatner, Leonard Nimoy, and DeForrest Kelly, appeared in 1966 and lasted three seasons. The show proved less than a smashing success in the ratings department, but each time cancellation was mentioned, hundreds of thousands of fan letters changed NBC's collective mind. To be sure, the show was a good one—still in syndication—but it hardly deserved the cult developed in its wake. The characterizations are excellent—Shatner's confident, free-wheeling, strong-willed Captain Kirk, Nimoy's "cute-eared" and logical Mr. Spock, and Kelly's nudgy but big-hearted physician "Bones"—and it is around these, and not the often mundane plots, that the cult seems to have formed. Annual *Star Trek* conventions in New York City draw eight to ten thousand devoted "trekkies."

Captain Nice (with William Daniels, the John Adams in Jack L. Warner's *1776,* Alice Ghostly, and Anne Prentiss as Candy Kane) and *Mr. Terrific,* with John McGiver, lasted half a season each in 1967. Buck Henry's *Captain Nice,* despite low ratings, being one of the most cleverly written shows in television history. ("Look! It's the man who flies around like an eagle. Look! It's the enemy of all that's illegal. Who can he be, this man with arms built like hammers? It's just some nut who flys around in pajamas. That's no nut, boy; that's Captain Nice!" declares the title music.

Another air-borne—and flighty—character came to the tube in 1967—*The Flying Nun,* an undeservedly long-lived program starring Sally Field, the daughter of Jock Mahoney.

Patrick McGoohan's *The Prisoner,* one of the finest series in television history and ostensibly a follow-up to *Secret Agent* with McGoohan (an exgovernment agent) kidnapped and sent to "the Village" to supply the "enemy" with information, premiered in 1968. The Village is that impersonal system of which we are all prisoners. McGoohan is referred to as Number Six in the series, a label about which he says, "I am not a number! I am a free man!" Despite its often profound and mature presentations, the British series was dropped after sixteen episodes.

A tip of the hat must go to Irwin Allen, whose various series—*Voyage to the Bottom of the Sea* (1964), with Richard Basehart and David Hedison; *Lost in Space* (1965), with Guy Williams (Disney's Zorro), June Lockhart, and Jonathan Harris; *Time Tunnel* (1967), with James Darren, Robert Colbert, Lee Meriwether, and Whit Bissell; and *Land of the Giants* (1968), with Gary Conway and Kurt Kasznar—provided always-entertaining episodes, not to mention garnering admirable portions of the ratings audience. Fans of "serious" science fiction are inclined to derogate Allen's work because of its allegedly juvenile slant. However, that is what kept these series alive. Children could understand the simple, if far-fetched, plots; adults found the fanciful nature of the stories appealing. Not a lofty

Jim Danforth's stop-motion plant monster in the Counterweight *episode of* Outer Limits.

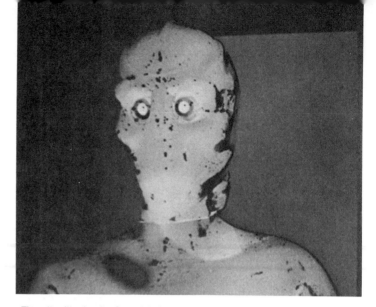

The pilot film for the Outer Limits *was* Galaxy Being, *in which Cliff Robertson transported this creature from Andromeda to Earth.*

excursion into the realm of "speculative fantasy," but firmly astride the steed of "science fiction," Mr. Allen's work always comes up with an hour's worth of entertainment. And that is what television should be.

On par with *Twilight Zone* as a consistently high-quality series was an incredible and costly show known as *The Outer Limits.* Produced by Joseph Stefano, the show premiered in 1963 and ran for two seasons. One is hard pressed to recall a bad episode. Technically, the show was incredible. Projects Unlimited—Jim Danforth, Wah Chang, and Gene Warren—was responsible for the show's astounding special effects. These included small, stop-motion animated creatures known as the Zanti Misfits (space ants with human faces), living tumbleweeds created to confound Eddie Albert, rocks that turned into crablike creatures, alien beings of every shape, size, and format imaginable, a man with a face of putty, robots, men evolved eons into the future, and so forth.

The series was also tops in scripting. The plots were fresh and exciting, and with rare exceptions when a moral or fable took center stage, they were all classic science fiction. The list of guest stars was also formidable. Martin Landau played a man from the future who, in fooling with the past, eliminated his birth; Cliff Robertson played a scientist who transported an antimatter being from the Andromeda galaxy to Earth; Leonard Nimoy played a reporter trying to clear a robot of murder in the "I, Robot" segment; and William Shatner portrayed an astronaut returned from Venus who, in "Cold Hands, Warm Heart," was unable to get warm. Robert Culp—later of *I Spy*— made several appearances including one as an Earthling mutated into alien form and another as a humanoid robot with a computer hand ("Demon with the Glass Hand," by Harlan Ellison). Whether *The Outer Limits* was simply too sophisticated or was in a poor time slot is difficult to say. The stories were not as gimmicky as those on *Twilight Zone*; also, the sixty-minute length may have been too much for most TV watchers. Whatever the reason, the loss of *The Outer Limits* was a severe blow to science fiction.

A less routine drama than most was *The Invaders* (1967), an underrated and well-made

Sally Field as The Flying Nun.

Roy Thinnes runs from the title creatures of the Quinn Martin teleseries The Invaders.

Van Williams (left) and Bruce Lee as the scientific crimefighters The Green Hornet *and Kato. From the ABC TV show.*

program on which, each week, Roy Thinnes tried to convince the world that human look-alikes had come to take over. One was able to distinguish Invaders, by the way, only because they were unable to bend their pinky fingers, or, in the case of black Invaders, their palms were black. Roy Thinnes was excellent as the confused savior of mankind, flashing a psychotic determination that is a peculiar aspect of his talent.

UFO (1972), from the husband-wife Anderson team of *Thunderbird* and *Journey to the Far Side of the Sun* fame, was an interesting syndicated made-in-England teleseries of the perpetual battle between SHADO (Supreme Headquarters Alien Defense Organization) and dangerous extraterrestrial would-be-invader enemies. The series featured excellent special effects and miniature models, as well as interesting subplots to the alien take-over attempts. One thoroughly impressive episode featured the death of SHADO Commander Straker's son and his subsequent divorce from his wife.

The last remaining inhabitant of the planet M-113, from the first Star Trek *show, entitled* The Man Trap.

The Cage *episode of* Star Trek *featured these pint-size intellectuals.*

Leonard Nemoy and William
Shatner as Mr. Spock and C
Kirk in Star Trek.

The starship Enterprise as se
in Star Trek.

The latest entry into the field is *Star Lost* (1973), a pretentious, absurd space opera that is part *Silent Running* (indeed, the series' effects are created by Doug Trumbull), part *2001: A Space Odyssey* (the show stars Keir Dullea), and part *Star Trek* (head writer Harlan Ellison was a contributor to—and critic—of the Gene Roddenberry *Star Trek*). The program—done on videotape, and sloppily at that—looks plastic and is poorly acted. It is pompous, mock-intelligentsia science fiction without *Star Trek's* flair or rapid tempo.

Feature-length science fiction has been a popular commodity in the network films-for-television grab-bag. Jack Palance starred in a fine adaptation of *Dr. Jekyll and Mr. Hyde* in 1968. *The Immortal,* a man with Olympian blood, was a feature-length one-shot before

206

becoming a short-lived series during the 1970 season. Gene Roddenberry gave us *Genesis Two,* the gimmick here being not the pointed ears of Spock, but rather, the dual navels of all the futuristic principals. *The Six Million Dollar Man* went from made-for-TV film to series in 1973. That one's about a man's head on a mechanical body.

Irwin Allen's *City beneath the Sea* was a potential successor to *Voyage to the Bottom of the Sea,* a good film about an experimental underwater superscience city governed by Stewart Whitman. For the film, Whitman must overcome a saboteur portrayed by Robert Wagner. *The Stranger* was an astronaut stranded on a planet in Earth orbit on the opposite side of the sun. The only difference between Earth and this other world—Terra—was that the Terran equivalent to the United States was living under a dictatorship. And then there was Robert Culp as an Arctic scientist who battled a strange extrasensory force in a lonely outpost for *A Cold Night's Death.*

One particularly abysmal aspect of TV science fiction is the awful Saturday-morning cartoon fare featuring such plagues as *Space Ghost, Journey to the Center of the Earth, Superman, Amazing Spider-Man, Fantastic Four, The Funky Phantom,* and so on, ad nauseum. These series, done in jerky "pseudo-animation," are a disgrace to both

207

Mr. Spock from Star Trek.

television and the animators responsible for such unprofessional work. Truly, gone are the days of entertaining children's programming such as the interestingly appointed *Space Angel, Supercar* . . . and *Captain Video,* where it all began.

Television watchers are inclined to look at the old live-action *Superman* reruns, compare them with a show like *Star Lost,* and claim in all innocence, "We've come a long way since then."

I cannot agree.

We have surrendered the imagination that spiced such mature showpieces as *Forbidden Planet* and *The Thing* for the pretentious pessimism of the "great, brooding thinkers" who tell us there's no hope for man. "(Mankind) must go on, conquest beyond conquest," said Oswald Cabal in *Things to Come.* With the world of today moving as it is, breakneck and free, there is no *time* to brood and reflect on man's inherent weaknesses. For only by his strengths—and not by his failings—will man carry himself through this day and into tomorrow.

Summing Up

Science fiction is constantly changing. By nature, the genre will always stay two steps ahead of the contemporary world and technology. Yet with man's geometrical progress, this is becoming increasingly difficult. In what direction will science fiction move? Indeed, is the label *science fiction* valid, or should the term *speculative fantasy,* a catch phrase of the realm's contemporary "thinkers," be adopted? These questions are, of course, rhetorical and of no concern to the masses of theatergoers and the average science-fiction fan. But it is interesting to examine the varied aspects of contemporary science fiction.

Noted science-fiction author Fred Hoyle is foremost on the list of writers whose fiction is based firmly in cold, scientific reason; on the opposite end of the scale is Canadian author Augustine Funnell, whose work probes the mind and soul of man as it responds to the fantastic.

Up-and-coming filmmakers like Ric Meyers, of Animated Industries, are busy establishing new trends in filmed science fiction. Meyers' *I Cynthian Love*—the story of a blinded astronaut's struggle to survive in space—is the most impressive science-fiction film since *2001: A Space Odyssey.* Douglas Trumbull's *Pyramid* promises to be a fine and substantial work, and the novels of Asimov, Clarke, Bradbury, and Heinlein will doubtless be brought to life by filmmakers with an eye for the fantastic.

Ray Harryhausen—despite threats to retire should his film *Sinbad's Golden Voyage* be given the same treatment by distributors as *Valley of Gwangi*—will be around, we hope, for centuries to come. And as long as Forry Ackerman–James Warren *Famous Monsters of Filmland* and Fred Clarke's *Cinefantastique* exist, the studio-public relationship will be kept firm, the lines of communication open. Indeed, much of the success of the monster business in the sixties was due to the Ackerman–Warren magazine—first of the film-monster publications and still, for the market at which it's aimed, the best of its type.

A featured performer said in and of *The Thing,* "An intellectual carrot? The mind boggles!" And as thus it will always be in the realm of science fiction. For making the unreal real is what science fiction is all about. And is that not, in fact, what man is all about?

The *Invasion of the Saucer Men is none other than a visit from space by these big-headed little bems.*

After the destruction of Metaluna, Jeff Morrow returns his prisoners to earth. From This Island Earth.

The Best and The Worst

The following motion pictures represent the best and the worst efforts in science-fiction film-history. The films here listed are those most commonly and readily available to the public via television and theatrical reissue. The critical comments accompanying each film have been capsulized from the body of the text for easy reference.

Abbott and Costello Go to Mars (1953)
Starring Bud Abbott, Lou Costello, Martha Hyer, Horace McMahon.
The comedy team heads for Venus but lands on Mars. The film is awful.

Absent-Minded Professor (1960)
Starring Fred MacMurray, Nancy Olson, Keenan Wynn, Tommy Kirk.
Disney veteran Robert Stevenson directed this entertaining fantasy about a rubberlike antigravity substance.

Aelita (1924)
Starring Igor Ilinsky, Yulia Salontsena, Kikolai Tseretelly.
Classic Russian science fiction story of the first men on mars. Lavish production values.

Alligator People (1959)
Starring Beverly Garland, George Macready, Lon Chaney, Jr.
Fair story of scientist who injects people with potion derived from bodies of alligators. Good makeup.

Alphaville (1965)
Starring Eddie Constantine, Anna Karina, Howard Vernon, Akim Tamiroff.
Jean-Luc Godard's comic-book world of Alphaville is a complete disappointment. Interesting set design; acting is poor.

Amazing Colossal Man (1957)
Starring Glenn Langan, Cathy Downs, Larry Thor.
Bert I. Gordon's tale of a fifty-foot-tall man features a sensitive performance by Glenn Langan as the Colossal Man. Special effects are abysmal.

Amazing Transparent Man (1960)
Starring Marguerite Chapman, Douglas Kennedy, James Griffith.
Veteran Edgar G. Ulmer's horrid Invisible Man film. One of the worst pictures ever made.

Andromeda Strain (1971)
Starring Arthur Hill, James Olson, David Wayne, Kate Reid.
Robert Wise directed this superb science-fiction film of a deadly bacterium brought to Earth by an American satellite. Exciting, well acted, and brilliantly directed.

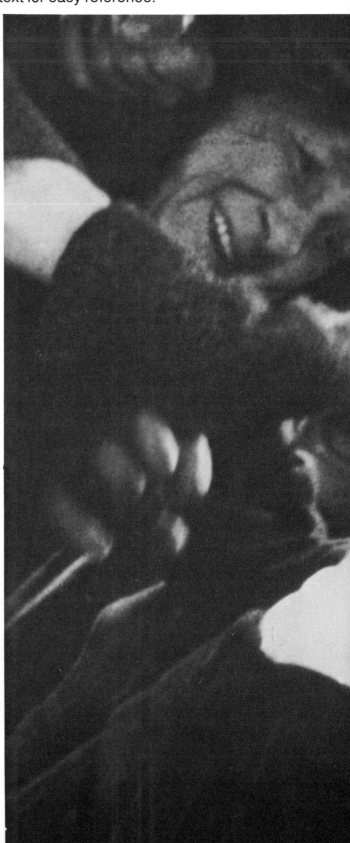

A gang of beggars descends upon Malcolm McDowell, who cannot fight back. He has been scientifically conditioned to be unable to perform acts of violence. From A Clockwork Orange.

Angry Red Planet (1959)
Starring Gerald Mohr, Nora Hayden, Les Tremayne, Jack Kruschen.
Ib Melchier's disappointing Cinemagic effort features an average script with below-average production values.

Around the World Under the Sea (1966)
Starring Lloyd Bridges, David McCallum, Shirley Eaton, Keenan Wynn.
Ex-second unit director Andrew Marton's unspectacular update of Jules Verne. Good cast wasted.

Atomic Submarine (1959)
Starring Arthur Franz, Dick Foran, Brett Halsey.
Spencer Bennet—director of *Atom Man vs. Superman*— does a far superior job with this film, the story of a cyclopean invader from space.

Atom Man vs. Superman (1949)
Starring Kirk Alyn, Lyle Talbot, Noel Neill, Tommy Bond.
Simple-minded adaptation of the Siegel-Schuster comic book. Technically inept and disappointing.

Malcolm McDowell mugs it up for authorities after his capture in A Clockwork Orange.

Attack of the Crab Monsters (1957)
Starring Richard Garland, Pamela Duncan, Russell Johnson.
Roger Corman's monsters-on-a-lost-island effort. Silly and contrived, with plastic-looking crab monsters assuming personalities of the dead.

Attack of the Fifty Foot Woman (1958)
Starring Allison Hayes, William Hudson, Yvette Vickers.
Bert I. Gordon and Nathan Juran's unintentionally comedic classic. If not looked upon as a science-fiction satire, the film is awful.

Battle Beneath the Earth (1968)
Starring Kerwin Mathews, Viviane Ventura, Robert Ayres.
Red China burrows beneath North America. Could have been great entertainment; instead, the film is sluggish and inexpertly acted.

Battle for the Planet of the Apes (1973)
Starring Roddy McDowall, Natalie Trundy.
Fifth film in the series and an absolute bore.

Battle in Outer Space (1960)
Starring Ryo Ikebe, Kyoko Anzai, Leonard Stanford.
Inoshiro Honda's superb Japan-battles-invaders film. Excellent special effects and a literate script make the difference.

Beast from Twenty Thousand Fathoms (1953)
Starring Paul Christian, Kenneth Tobey, Paula Raymond.
Eugene Lourie's direction and Ray Harryhausen's special effects spice Ray Bradbury's inventive screenplay about a prehistoric beast running rampant in New York City.

Beast with a Million Eyes (1955)
Starring Paul Birch, Lorna Thayer.
Modest Roger Corman thriller of a mind-possessing invader from space.

Before I Hang (1941)
Starring Boris Karloff, Evelyn Keyes, Bruce Bennet.
Karloff finds a cure for death.

Beginning of the End (1957)
Starring Peter Graves, Peggie Castle, Morris Ankrum.
Bert I. Gordon's engrossing tale of grasshoppers invading Chicago. Fine performances, good script, awful special effects.

Beneath the Planet of the Apes (1970)
Starring James Franciscus, Linda Harrison, Kim Hunter, Maurice Evans.
Solid sequel to Planet of the Apes, second in the series. Guest star Charlton Heston and James Franciscus detonate atomic warhead and blow up the planet. Entertaining.

Beyond the Time Barrier (1960)
Starring Robert Clarke, Darlene Tompkins, Arienne Arden.
Edgar G. Ulmer's modest journey into the future. Not bad.

Black Scorpion (1957)
Starring Richard Denning, Mara Corday, Mario Navarro.
Special effects by Willis O'Brien are the highlight of an otherwise routine monster-on-the-loose film. Mexican settings add color.

The Blob (1958)
Starring Steve McQueen, Aneta Corseaut, Earl Rowe.
Excellent special effects and fine photography are better than this silly thriller deserves; Steve McQueen is awful.

Blood Beast from Outer Space (1964)
Starring John Saxon.
Modest tale of man who kidnaps Earth girls and sends them to Jupiter. Atmospheric, well-acted.

Brain from Planet Arous (1958)
Starring John Agar, Joyce Meader, Robert Fuller.
Nathan Juran's above-average story of a space brain intent on conquering the universe. Agar shines; the scene shot through a water-cooler is best.

Breaking the Sound Barrier (1952)
Starring Ralph Richardson, Ann Todd, Nigel Patrick.
David Lean's meticulous and excellent story of the development of the supersonic jet plane. Superb.

Bride of Frankenstein (1935)
Starring Boris Karloff, Elsa Lanchester, Colin Clive, Ernest Thesiger.
Director James Whale's superior sequel to *Frankenstein*. The film is flawless; sequence with the blind man and the monster is brilliant.

Buck Rogers (1939)
Starring Buster Crabbe, Constance Moore, Jackie Moran.
Fine adaptation of the comic strip. Crabbe and special effects are stars.

Catwomen of the Moon (1953)
Starring Sonny Tufts.
One of the all-time disasters.

A Clockwork Orange (1971)
Starring Malcolm McDowell, Adrienne Cori, Patrick Magee.
Stanley Kubrick's classic of the near future.

Colossus of New York (1958)
Starring John Baragrey, Mala Powers, Otto Kruger.
Eugene Lourie's above-average story of a man's brain in a robot's body. Well worth watching.

Conquest of Space (1955)
Starring Walter Brooke, Eric Fleming, William Hopper, Ross Martin.
Disappointing George Pal–Byron Haskin effort; even special effects are below par.

Conquest of the Planet of the Apes (1972)
Starring Roddy McDowall, Natalie Trundy, Don Murray.
The finest of the four sequels, as apes rebel against human oppression and take over the world in the 1990s. Filmed in Los Angeles' Century City complex.

Crack in the World (1965)
Starring Dana Andrews, Janette Scott, Kieron Moore.

Andrew Marton's excellent end-of-the-world film. Strong performances and special effects; surprise ending.

Crawling Eye (1958)
Starring Forrest Tucker, Janet Munro.
Enormous tentacled orbs from space; tense, well acted.

Creature from the Black Lagoon (1954)
Starring Richard Carlson, Julia Adams, Richard Denning.
Director Jack Arnold's classic tale of the amphibious gill man. Dynamic, brutal, and well done.

Creature Walks among Us (1956)
Starring Jeff Morrow, Rex Reason, Leigh Snowden.
Third in the Creature series; experiments make the Creature more human. Impressive.

Creeping Unknown (1956)
Starring Brian Donlevy, Margia Dean, Jack Warner.
Astronaut turns into a slithering mass; superb entertainment.

Curse of Frankenstein (1957)
Starring Peter Cushing, Christopher Lee.
Colorful retelling of the original Shelley *Frankenstein*. Solid performances; fine technical effects in all but makeup, which is not up to the Karloff original.

Daleks: Invasion Earth 2150 A.D. (1966)
Starring Peter Cushing, Bernard Cribbins, Andrew Kier.
Modest thriller about an invasion of London by robotized aliens. Tongue in cheek; Cushing is, as usual, superb.

Day Mars Invaded Earth (1963)
Starring Kent Taylor.
Fine film of electrical beings from Mars; for once the Martians win.

Day of the Triffids (1963)
Starring Howard Keel, Janette Scott, Kieron Moore.
Fine film adaptation of the John Wyndham novel. Modest technical effects; good script and cast.

Day the Earth Caught Fire (1962)
Starring Edward Judd, Janet Munro, Leo McKern.
Tense thriller as Earth starts moving closer to the sun. Solid performances; fine effort.

Day the Earth Stood Still (1951)
Starring Michael Rennie, Patricia Neal, Hugh Marlowe.
Classic Robert Wise film wherein outer-space emissary visits Earth to order a halt in atomic experimentation. A flawless film.

Deadly Mantis (1957)
Starring Craig Stevens, William Hopper, Alix Talton.
Below-average script and abysmal special effects ruin a potentially good effort from veteran director Nathan Juran.

Destination: Inner Space (1966)
Starring Scott Brady, Sheree North, Gary Merrill, Wende Wagner.
Low budget and average performances do not prevent director Francis Lyon from providing a first-rate entertainment. Nothing profound; just fun.

Destination Moon (1950)
Starring John Archer, Warner Anderson, Tom Powers.
Good pioneer effort from Producer George Pal. Fine
special effects and art direction; good script.

Devil Commands (1941)
Starring Boris Karloff, Amanda Duff, Richard Fiske.
Edward Dmytryk's all-right mad-scientist film. Karloff
tries to communicate with the dead, causes much
unhappiness along the way.

Dr. Strangelove—or How I Learned to Stop Worrying and Love the Bomb (1964)
Starring Peter Sellers, George C. Scott, Sterling Hayden,
Keenan Wynn.
Stanley Kubrick's World War III black-humor classic. On
target and perfect.

Dr. Who and the Daleks (1966)
Starring Peter Cushing, Roy Castle, Jennie Linden.
Another feature film edited from the British television
series. Fun; a bit juvenile, but not bad. Cushing is great.

Dr. X (1932)
Starring Lionel Atwill, Fay Wray, Preston Foster, Lee
Tracy.
Excellent mystery of mad strangler. Mood, acting, and
script are all top notch.

Donovan's Brain (1953)
Starring Lew Ayres, Gene Evans, Nancy Olson, Steve
Brodie.
Merely average story of millionaire's brain kept alive in a
modified fish tank. Could have been much better.

Earth vs. the Flying Saucers (1956)
Starring Hugh Marlowe, Joan Taylor, Morris Ankrum,
Donald Curtis.
Average invasion-from-space film featuring
unbelieveably good Ray Harryhausen special effects.
The battle royal between Earthmen and saucers in
Washington, D.C., is incredible.

Enemy from Space (1957)
Starring Brian Donlevy, Michael Ripper, Sidney James.
Good invaders-from-space film, the second in the
Professor Quatermass series.

Escape from the Planet of the Apes (1971)
Starring Kim Hunter, Sal Mineo, Roddy McDowall.
Apes escape from doomed planet and land in Southern
California, circa 1973. The third in the series.

Evil of Frankenstein (1964)
Starring Peter Cushing, Duncan Lamont, Kiwi Kingston.
Not-bad Hammer film, the third in their Frankenstein
series. Good production values; solid acting.

Fahrenheit 451 (1966)
Starring Julie Christie, Oskar Werner, Anton Diffring.
Director Francois Truffaut's adaptation of the Ray
Bradbury novel. Well-made and not without impact.

Malcolm McDowell as the vicious Alex, leaving the Korova Milkbar in a scene from A Clockwork Orange. *In this bar, one may purchase milk spiked with mescaline.*

Fail Safe (1964)
   Starring Henry Fonda, Walter Matthau, Fritz Weaver.
   Disappointing film based on the so-so best seller. Fonda
   is fine; he's no Peter Sellers, though.

Fantastic Voyage (1966)
   Starring Raquel Welch, Stephen Boyd, Donald
   Pleasence, Arthur Kennedy.
   Overrated, overblown, and pretentious. Director Richard
   Fleisher has been in much better form.

Fire Maidens of Outer Space (1956)
   Starring Anthony Dexter, Swan Shaw, Paul Carpenter,
   Jacqueline Curti.
   Unsophisticated, silly, and yet . . . thoroughly enjoyable.

First Spaceship on Venus (1960)
   Starring Yoko Tani, Oldrich Lukes, Ignacy Machowski.
   Fine production values and convincing special effects
   highlight an otherwise hackneyed science-fiction thriller.

Five (1951)
   Starring William Phipps, Susan Douglas, James
   Anderson, Earl Lee.
   Innovative author-filmmaker Arch Oboler turns in a
   gripping, original film of postwar mores, survival, and
   interpersonal relationships. The best film ever of this
   sort.

Five Million Years to Earth (1967)
   Starring James Donald, Andrew Keir, Barbara Shelley.
   Excellent film—the third in the Quatermass series—
   about the discovery of a five-million-year-old Martian
   spaceship buried beneath London streets. Excellent
   special effects, acting, and directing.

Flame Barrier (1958)
   Starring Arthur Franz, Kathleen Crowley, Robert Brown.
   Interesting and inventive tale of a mysterious satellite in
   the African jungle.

Flash Gordon (1936)
   Starring Buster Crabbe, Jean Rogers, Frank Shannon,
   Charles Middleton.
   The comic strip comes to life; Crabbe, Middleton, and
   special effects are great!

Flash Gordon Conquers the Universe (1940)
   Starring Buster Crabbe, Charles Middleton.
   Third Flash Gordon film; boring, silly, and entirely
   without merit.

Flash Gordon's Trip to Mars (1938)
   Starring Buster Crabbe, Jean Rogers, Charles
   Middleton, Frank Shannon.
   Fine sequel to *Flash Gordon;* maintains quality of the
   original while our hero moves to save Earth from the
   clutches of Ming the Merciless.

The Fly (1958)
   Starring David Hedison, Patricia Owens, Vincent Price.
   A classic. Man becomes half-fly during mixup in
   scientific experiment. Frightening and thoroughly
   convincing; only Price is a letdown.

*Sinbad attacks the monstrous
cyclops in the opening minutes of*
The Seventh Voyage of Sinbad.

Flying Disc Man from Mars (1950)
Starring Walter Reed, Lois Collier, Greg Gay. Average science fiction serial. Mota the Martian plants his outer-space buggy in a volcano; by chapter twelve the mountain erupts, destroying the menace.

Forbidden Planet (1956)
Starring Walter Pidgeon, Anne Francis, Leslie Nielsen, Brilliant story of an Earth saucer battling the Monster from the Id on planet Altair-Four. One of the best . . . if not *the* best.

The Forbin Project (1970)
Starring Eric Braeden, Susan Clark, Gordon Pinsent. Omnipotent computer takes over; contemporary thriller is timely and well done.

The 4-D Man (1959)
    Starring Robert Lansing, Lee Meriwether, James Congdon.
    Effective story of a man who can pass through solid matter. Lansing shines, as usual.

4-Sided Triangle (1953)
    Starring Stephen Murray, Barbara Payton.

Barbarella in an aviary torture chamber.

So-so effort from Hammer. Experiments to duplicate living people.

Frankenstein (1931)
    Starring Boris Karloff, Colin Clive, Dwight Frye.
    James Whale's masterpiece. Jack Pierce's makeup and Karloff's masterful performance stand out; sets, photography, and script are perfect.

Frankenstein 1970 (1958)
    Starring Boris Karloff, Tom Dugan, Jana Lund.
    Karloff as Dr. Frankenstein. Awful.

From the Earth to the Moon (1958)
    Starring Joseph Cotten, Debra Paget, George Sanders.
    Brilliant cast wasted by Byron Haskin's pitiful adaptation of Jules Verne classic. How any director could have botched this one is beyond belief.

Gamma People (1956)
    Starring Paul Douglas, Eva Bartok, Walter Rilla.
    Communist efforts to robotize human beings. Interesting, though hardly definitive.

Ghidrah, the Three-headed Monster (1965)
    Starring Yosuke Natsuki, Uuriko Hoshi, Emi Ito.
    Another Inoshiro Honda monster on the loose. Excellent special effects and a clever script highlight an otherwise routine monsterama.

Giant Behemoth (1958)
    Starring Andre Morell, Gene Evans, Leigh Madison.
    Eugene Lourie directs; Willis O'Brien animates; yet, the film is not what it should have been. Evans and Morell are superb.

Giant Claw (1957)
    Starring Jeff Morrow, Mara Corday, Morris Ankrum.
    Giant bird from space. He should have stayed there.

Giant Gila Monster (1959)
    Starring Don Sullivan, Lisa Simone, Shug Fisher.
    Worse than the *Giant Claw*. Never thought it was possible.

Gigantis, the Fire Monster (1959)
    Starring Hiroshi Koizumi, Setsuko Makayama, Midru Chiaki.
    American version of *Godzilla Raids Again* pits the fire-breathing dinosaur against Anzilla, and guess who wins. Not bad at all.

Girl in the Moon (1929)
    Starring Gerda Maurus, Willy Fritsch, Fritz Rasp.
    Director Fritz Lang's second science-fiction film. Finest of all trips to the moon.

Godzilla, King of the Monsters (1955)
    Starring Raymond Burr, Takashi Shimura, Momoko Kochi.
    Excellent, frightening, and first of the Japanese monsters on the loose. Eiji Tsuburaya's special effects shine; Inoshiro Honda's original (before added American sequences) was brilliant. Best of this type.

Gog (1954)
Starring Richard Egan, Constance Dowling, Herbert Marshall.
Alien craft spies on underground U.S. space center. Fine, convincing effort.

Gorgo (1961)
Starring Bill Travers, William Sylvester, Vincent Winter.
Eugene Lourie's finest monster film.Excellent color and special effects highlight tale of beast that decimates London in search of kidnapped child.

Green Slime (1969)
Starring Robert Horton, Luciana Paluzzi, Ted Gunther, Bud Widom.
Glop-people on American space station. Terrible.

Have Rocket Will Travel (1959)
Starring the Three Stooges, Jerome Cowan, Bob Colbert.
Moe, Larry, and Curly-Joe on Venus. Juvenile but fun.

I Married a Monster from Outer Space (1958)
Starring Tom Tryon, Gloria Talbott, Ken Lynch.
Very effective tale of a woman who marries the alien monster masquerading as her husband. Awful title; great film!

Just two of the super-scientific menaces that threaten Barbarella on her merry romp throughout the universe. And what she won't do to save the United States from destruction!

Incredible Shrinking Man (1957)

Starring Grant Williams, Randy Stuart, April Kent.
Jack Arnold's classic tale adapted from Richard
Matheson's brilliant novel.
Man cannot stop shrinking after passing through strange
mist. Williams is fine; special effects are superlative.

Invaders from Mars (1953)

Starring Helena Carter, Arthur Franz, Jimmy Hunt, Leif
Erickson.
Director William Cameron Menzies creates a truly
memorable nightmare when a young boy wakes up in the
middle of the night to witness the arrival of a flying
saucer. Low, low budget; high-quality film.

Invasion of the Body Snatchers (1956)

Starring Kevin McCarthy, Dana Wynter, Larry Gates,
Carolyn Jones.
Excellent film version of the Jack Finney novel. Don
Siegel's directing is completely expert, and the film is a
pleasure to behold.

Invasion of the Saucer Men (1957)

Starring Steve Terrell, Frank Gorshin, Ed Nelson.
Above-average goings-on, with midget invaders versus
teenagers.

Invasion of the Star Creatures (1964)

Starring Bob Ball, Frankie Ray, Dolores Reed.
Corny tale as pair of soldiers thwart invasion of beautiful
girls and humanoid carrots.

Invisible Boy (1957)

Starring Richard Eyer, Diane Brewster, Harold J. Stone.
Forbidden Planet's Robby the Robot is back . . . this time
as a kidnapper. Boy is abducted and sent to space; film
is so-so.

Invisible Man (1933)

Starring Claude Rains, Gloria Stuart, Una O'Connor.
James Whale and another of his classics. H. G. Wells
story gets prime treatment from director Whale and
special-effects man John P. Fulton. Brilliant.

Island of Lost Souls (1933)

Starring Charles Laughton, Bela Lugosi, Richard Arlen.
Effective translation of H. G. Wells' *Island of Dr. Moreau*
to screen. Laughton and makeup are superb.

It Came from Beneath the Sea (1955)

Starring Kenneth Tobey, Faith Domergue, Donald Curtis.
Harryhausen's five-tentacled octopus. Without the
special effects, it would be nothing.

It Conquered the World (1956)

Starring Peter Graves, Beverly Garland, Lee Van Cleef.
Creature from Venus; movie from hunger.

It! The Terror from beyond Space (1958)

Starring Marshall Thompson, Shawn Smith, Kim
Spaulding.
Martian monster stowaway on American spaceship. Lots
of excitement; Ray Corrigan is a terrifying Martian.

Journey to the Center of the Earth (1959)

Starring James Mason, Arlene Dahl, Pat Boone.
Excellent, fun-filled adaptation of the Verne classic. Fine
performances; superb sets and special effects.

Original ad art for The Day the
Earth Stood Still.

Journey to the Far Side of the Sun (1969)
   Starring Roy Thinnes, Ian Hendry, Patrick Wymark, Lynn Loring.
   Confusing but colorful story of an astronaut landing on planet in Earth orbit on the opposite side of the sun. Superb special effects.

Journey to the Seventh Planet (1962)
   Starring John Agar, Greta Thyssen, Ann Smyrner.
   Interesting, off-beat trip to Uranus. Once again, special effects are the star.

Just Imagine (1930)
   Starring John Garrick, Maureen O'Sullivan, El Brendel.
   Filmmakers' prediction of 1980. Worth a look; not up to *Metropolis.*

Killers from Space (1953)
   Starring Peter Graves, James Seay, Barbara Bestar.
   Bug-eyed monsters in leotards versus Peter Graves. Audience loses.

King Dinosaur (1955)
   Starring Bill Bryant, Wanda Curtis, Douglas Henderson, Patti Gallagher.
   Bert I. Gordon production about a trip to the planet Nova. Crude and unconvincing.

King Kong vs. Godzilla (1963)
   Starring James Yagi, Michael Keith, Tadao Takashima.
   The special effects are good, and the color is nice . . . but that's it. The film is an insult to the good name of Kong.

King of the Rocket Men (1949)
   Starring Tristram Coffin, Mae Clarke, Don Haggerty, I. Stanford Jolley.
   Not-bad serial about crime fighter with jet-propelled rocket suit. Excellent special effects make for impressive flying sequences.

Konga (1961)
   Starring Michael Gough, Margo Johns, Jess Conrad, Claire Gordon.
   Gough is fine as mad professor lusting for shapely student; the rest of the film is a bore.

Kronos (1957)
   Starring Jeff Morrow, Barbara Lawrence, Morris Ankrum.
   Awesome monster robot from space drains Earth of all atomic and electrical power. Atmospheric, convincing, and expert.

Man from Planet X (1951)
   Starring Robert Clarke, Margaret Field, Ray Bond.
   An atmospheric and well-made film from Edgar G. Ulmer. Android creature visits Earth, an advance scout for invasion forces. One of the better invasion-of-earth entries.

Man-Made Monster (1941)
   Starring Lionel Atwill, Lon Chaney, Jr., Anne Nagel.
   Chaney gets superstrength from electric charges. Just average.

The Manster (1961)
   Starring Peter Dyneley, Jane Hylton.
   Okay Jekyll-Hyde variation from Japan.

Rare original poster ad art from King Kong.

223

Man They Could Not Hang (1939)
Starring Boris Karloff, Lorna Gray, Robert Wilcox, Ann Doran, Roger Pryor.
Karloff conquers death, again.

Man with Nine Lives (1940)
Starring Boris Karloff, Roger Pryor, Jo Ann Sayers, Stanley Brown.
And once more, it's Karloff versus death. Modest mad-doctor epic.

Man with the X-ray Eyes (1963)
Starring Ray Milland, Harold J. Stone, Diana Van Der Vlis.
Scathing tale of scientist who keeps seeing deeper and deeper into the tangible world. Trite in spots but effective and well-done.

Marooned (1970)
Starring Gregory Peck, Gene Hackman, David Janssen, James Franciscus.
John Sturges' thoroughly disappointing disaster. Nothing works—not the script, special effects, or acting. A complete disaster, save for breathtaking shots of an Apollo–Saturn-5 launch at the beginning of the film.

Metropolis (1925)
Starring Brigitte Helm, Alfred Abel, Gustav Froehlich, Rudolf Klein-Rogge.
Fritz Lang's masterpiece. Story of futuristic city and the tension created by its caste system. One of the greats.

Missile to the Moon (1959)
Starring Richard Travis, Cathy Downs, K. T. Stevens, Tommy Cook.
Low-grade entertainment; some interesting moments.

Monolith Monsters (1957)
Starring Grant Williams, Lola Albright.
Excellent film of rocks from space that grow to monster size.

Monster That Challenged the World (1957)
Starring Tim Holt, Audrey Dalton, Hans Conreid.
Adequate monster-from-the-ocean-floor saga; better than most.

Moon Zero-Two (1969)
Starring James Olson, Adrienne Cori, Catherina Von Schell.
The first space Western. Cute idea falls flat.

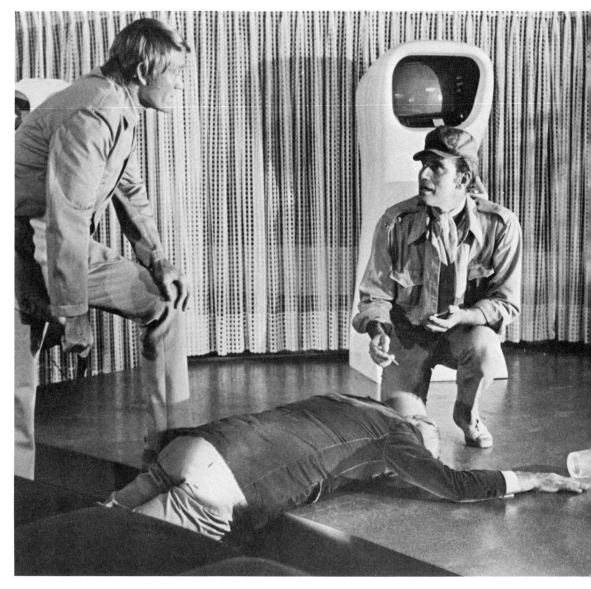

People scoopers disperse a rowdy crowd in a tense scene from Soylent Green.

Charlton Heston questions an "innocent" Chuck Conners about the death of Joseph Cotten in the futuristic Soylent Green.

Mothra (1962)
Starring Franky Sakai, Hiroshi Koizumi, Hyoko Hagawa, Jelly Itoh.
Inoshiro Honda's beautiful monster moth. Graceful, tasteful, and magnificent.

Mouse on the Moon (1963)
Starring Terry-Thomas, Margaret Rutherford, Ron Moody, Bernard Cribbens.
Hilarious goings-on in Grand Fenwick as Duchy goes to the moon.

Mysterious Dr. Satan (1940)
Starring Eduardo Cianelli, Robert Wilcox, William Newell.
Above-average serial thriller, simple-minded as most.

Mysterious Island (1964)
Starring Gary Merrill, Percy Herbert, Michael Craig, Joan Greenwood.
Excellent version of Verne's sequel to Twenty Thousand Leagues under the Sea. Cast is okay; Herbert Lom's Captain Nemo, Bernard Herrmann's music, and Ray Harryhausen's special effects are exquisite.

1984 (1956)
Starring Edmund O'Brien, Michael Redgrave, Jan Sterling.
Disappointing screen version of the Orwell classic.

Nutty Professor (1963)
Starring Jerry Lewis, Stella Stevens, Howard Morris.
Warm, funny, and sensitive semicomedic retelling of the Jekyll-Hyde story. Lewis is meek college professor who becomes "Joe Cool" after imbibing formula. Lewis's best, and that says a lot.

Omega Man (1971)
Starring Charlton Heston, Anthony Zerbe, Rosalind Cash.
Heston is wasted in a weak adaptation of Richard Matheson's I Am Legend. Vampires take over the Earth; Heston is the last "normal" human being. Effective in spots but generally disappointing.

On the Beach (1959)
Starring Gregory Peck, Ava Gardner, Fred Astaire, Anthony Perkins.
Lukewarm filming of Nevil Shute's potent novel. Stanley Kramer tries hard with a talky script, but the film is better left alone with its striking visuals.

Panic in the Year Zero (1962)
Starring Ray Milland, Jean Hagan, Frankie Avalon, Richard Garland.
A Milland-directed post–World War III film. Not bad.

Phantom Creeps (1939)
Starring Bela Lugosi, Robert Kent, Regis Toomey, Edward Van Sloan.
From Beebe and Goodkind, directors of *Buck Rogers,* comes a silly and childish film that wastes the talent of Bela Lugosi. Thrill-less serial of power-mad Lugosi and his hibernatory ray.

Phantom Empire (1935)
Starring Gene Autry, Frankie Darro, Betsy King Ross.
Well-made serial about subterranean Murania and its connection with Autry's Radio Ranch.

Phantom Planet (1961)
Starring Dean Fredericks, Coleen Gray, Francis X. Bushman.
Better-than-average film about astronaut who helps Rheton overcome the monster Solarites. Well directed by William Marshall.

Robert Duvall as the "deviant" THX-1138.

Robert Duvall attempts to escape his stifling life in the world of the future. From THX-1138.

James Olson attempts to prevent the destruction of an underground scientific complex in The Andromeda Strain. *In this sequence, lasar rays prevent his reentering a sealed chamber.*

Planet of the Apes (1968)
Starring Charlton Heston, Roddy McDowall, Kim Hunter, Maurice Evans.
Striking adaptation of Pierre Boulle's *Monkey Planet.* Heston superb as astronaut on a planet where apes rule and man is the slave. Directed by Franklin J. Schaffner, of *Patton* fame.

Plan Nine from Outer Space (1959)
Starring Bela Lugosi, Gregory Walcott, Lyle Talbot, Tor Johnson.
One of the great disasters. Lugosi's last film; zombies from space. Nonexistent budget; just plain garbage.

The Power (1967)
Starring George Hamilton, Michael Rennie, Earl Holliman, Suzanne Pleshette.
Staggering, wholly nightmarish film of supermind Adam Hart, who seeks to destory the members of a small scientific team. Magnificent all the way.

Purple Monster Strikes (1945)
Starring Roy Barcroft, Mary Moore.
Good serial. Barcroft is substanceless Martian who can enter and control the bodies of key figures in his plan to conquer the world.

Queen of Outer Space (1958)
Starring Zsa Zsa Gabor, Eric Fleming, Laurie Mitchell.
Scraping the bottom of the barrel. Venus plans to invade Earth; Fleming (of Earth) and Gabor (of Venus) put a stop to it. Makes *Missile to the Moon* look brilliant.

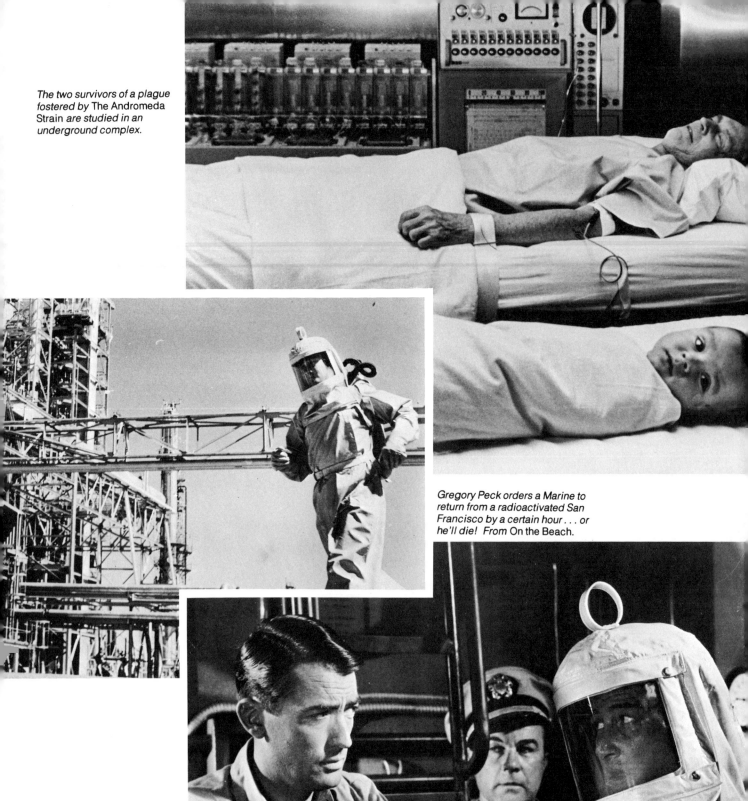

The two survivors of a plague fostered by The Andromeda Strain are studied in an underground complex.

Gregory Peck orders a Marine to return from a radioactivated San Francisco by a certain hour . . . or he'll die! From On the Beach.

Natalie Trundy is trussed-up in
Conquest of the Planet of the
Apes.

Radar Men from the Moon (1951)
Starring George Wallace, Clayton Moore, Aline Towne, Roy Barcroft.
So-so serial featuring Commando Cody.

Red Planet Mars (1952)
Starring Peter Graves, Andrea King, Marvin Miller.
God contacts man, reveals himself to be a Martian. Clever, if overcooked.

Reptilicus (1962)
Starring: Carl Ottosen, Ann Smyrner.
Worst of the monster-on-the-loose flicks.

Return of the Fly (1959)
Starring Vincent Price, Brett Halsey, David Frankham, Danielle De Metz.
Adequate sequel to *The Fly.* Some horrifying moments.

Revenge of the Creature (1955)
Starring John Agar, Lori Nelson, John Bromfield, Nestor Paiva.
Second Creature film, directed by Jack Arnold. Rather pointless.

Robinson Crusoe on Mars (1964)
Starring Paul Mantee, Vic Lundin, Adam West.
Excellent story of man stranded on Mars. Survival in hostile environment is explicitly detailed. Death Valley locations suffice as Martian surface.

Rocketship XM (1950)
Starring Lloyd Bridges, Osa Massen, Hugh O'Brien.
Adequate trip to Mars via the Moon. Made on a shoestring, but works due to disciplined direction by Kurt Neumann.

Rodan, the Flying Monster (1957)
Starring Kenji Sawara, Yumi Shirakawa, Akihiko Hirato.
Inoshiro Honda's twin pteranodons. Excellent special effects and exceptional finale are highlights.

Satan Bug (1965)
Starring George Maharis, Anne Francis, Richard Basehart, Dana Andrews.
Talky John Sturges film based on the novel by Alistair MacLean. Deadly bug is stolen from lab; film details efforts to retrieve it.

Apes batter Don Murray in their rebellion from Conquest of the Planet of the Apes.

Silent Running (1972)

Starring Bruce Dern, Cliff Potts, Ron Rivkin, Jesse Vint. Preachy star trek. Dern saves space station carrying last remnants of terrestrial plant life. Good special effects and miniatures; solid performance by Dern; intelligent script.

Slaughterhouse Five (1972)

Starring Michael Sacks, Ron Leibman, Eugene Roche. Sturdy version of Vonnegut novel. For connoisseurs of the author only.

Son of Frankenstein (1939)

Starring Boris Karloff, Lionel Atwill, Bela Lugosi, Basil Rathbone.
Lavish conclusion to the Karloff-born *Frankenstein* series. Excellent entertainment.

Soylent Green (1973)

Starring Charlton Heston, Edward G. Robinson, Chuck Conners, Joseph Cotten.
Dynamic, frightening vision of the future based on Harry Harrison's novel *Make Room, Make Room!* Population is out of control; food is a collector's item.

Space Children (1958)

Starring Michel Ray, Adam Williams, Peggy Webber, Jackie Coogan.
Director Jack Arnold's contribution to the brain-from-space genre. Extraterrestrial mind takes over kids to sabotage space-research center. Average.

Superman (1948)

Starring Kirk Alyn, Noel Neill, Tommy Bond, Carol Forman.
A lacking serial version of the far-famed comic-book hero. Alyn is fine enough; plot and special effects are not.

Superman and the Mole Men (1951)

Starring George Reeves, Phyllis Coates.
Reeves's debut as the Man of Steel. Better than the two serials; moderately entertaining.

Tarantula (1955)

Starring John Agar, Leo G. Carroll, Mara Corday.
Jack Arnold's giant bug. Impressive special effects and a good script elevate this one from obscurity.

Target Earth (1954)

Starring Richard Denning, Virginia Grey, Robert Ruark. Excellent story of people stranded in evacuated town after an invasion from space. Denning is sturdy; direction by Sherman Rose is taut.

Eris Braeden and Bradford Dillman (right) prepare to inject Roddy McDowall and Kim Hunter with truth serum in Escape from the Planet of the Apes.

Teenage Caveman (1959)
Starring Robert Vaughn.
Another post-World War III film from Roger Corman. Surprise ending and formula have since become trite. Story of cave people who are in reality what's left of man after atomic warfare. Some effective moments.

Teenagers from Outer Space (1959)
Starring David Love, Dawn Anderson, Harvey B. Dunn, Bryant Grant.
One of the five worst films ever made. The title says it all.

Terrornauts (1967)
Starring Charles Hawtrey.
Below-average story of Earthlings kidnapped to spaceship to help battle ruthless aliens. Low production values ruin potentially fine tale.

Them! (1954)
Starring James Whitmore, Edmund Gwenn, James Arness.
Best of the bug-monster films. Atomically mutated ants grown giant invade Los Angeles. Superb entertainment; fine performances by all.

These Are the Damned (1965)
Starring MacDonald Carey, Shirley Anne Field, Viveca Lindfors, Alexander Knox.
Excellent, gripping tale of children being raised to procreate in radiated society should the world engage in atomic warfare. Directed by Joseph Losey.

The Thing (1951)
Starring Kenneth Tobey, James Arness, Margaret Sheridan.
One of the all-time greats. Monster from space terrorizes an Arctic outpost. Directed by Christian Nyby, although many contend producer Howard Hawks performed the directorial chores.

Things to Come (1936)
Starring Raymond Massey, Ralph Richardson, Maurice Braddell.
H. G. Wells's look at the future. Brilliant; in a class by itself. Directed by William Cameron Menzies.

This Island Earth (1955)
Starring Jeff Morrow, Faith Domergue, Rex Reason.
Engrossing, special effects-ful film of scientists spirited to the planet Metaluna, a world at war with a neighboring planet. A perfect film.

Three Stooges in Orbit (1962)
Starring Carol Christensen, Edson Stroll, Emil Sitka.
Not as bad as it sounds. Some funny moments; some lousy moments; generally okay.

THX-1138 (1971)
Starring Donald Pleasence, Robert Duvall.
Intriguing look at a sterile, inhumane future. From George Lucas and Francis Ford Coppolla (director of *Godfather*).

The Time Machine (1960)
Starring Rod Taylor, Yvette Mimieux, Alan Young, Sebastian Cabot.
Entertaining fantasy from George Pal. Technically, the film is flawless; surely one of the better H. G. Wells adaptations.

Time Travelers (1964)
Starring Preston Foster, Philip Carey, Merry Anders, John Hoyt.
Soggy script and amateur theatrics ruin a potentially good tale of travel into the future.

Tobor the Great (1954)
Starring Charles Drake, Karin Booth, Billy Chapin.
Tobor . . . that's robot spelled backward. It's not the only thing that's backward in this feeble effort.

Transatlantic Tunnel (1935)
Starring Richard Dix, Madge Evans, Leslie Banks, James Carew.
Fine spectacle–science fiction detailing the building of a tunnel beneath the Atlantic Ocean. Entertaining; well made.

A Trip to the Moon (1903)
Starring Georges Mélies.
Directed by Melies, this is acknowledged the first major science fiction film. A cleverly mounted silent fantasy with emphasis on the visuals.

Twenty Million Miles to Earth (1957)
Starring William Hopper, Joan Taylor, Frank Puglia.
Average monster-from-space film highlighted by Ray Harryhausen's finest special-effects work to date. Technically, the film is incredible.

*tians wonder what's up
ng* The Three Stooges in
it.

Twenty Seventh Day (1957)
Starring Gene Barry, Valerie French, George Voscovec.
Good film marred by anti-Communist propaganda. Alien creature gives five human beings capsules, each with the capacity to destroy the world.

Twenty Thousand Leagues under the Sea (1954)
Starring Kirk Douglas, James Mason.
Excellent Disney version of the Jules Verne classic. Fine performances and astounding special effects, sets, and underwater photography.

The Twonky (1953)
Starring Hans Conried, Gloria Blondell, Trilby Conried.
Arch Oboler's clever satire of a living television set that plants itself in an American home and takes over minds. End sequence—when the dead TV "gives birth"—is a bit much to swallow . . . but it works nonetheless.

2001: A Space Odyssey (1968)
Starring Keir Dullea, Gary Lockwood, William Sylvester.
Now-classic Kubrick film of Earth's first contact with extraterrestrial life. Special effects are overrated, but the film as a whole is magnificent.

Undersea Kingdom (1936)
Starring Ray Corrigan, Lon Chaney ., Lane Chandler, Lois Wilde, Monte Blue.
Above-average serial wherein Atlantis makes preparations to conquer the surface world; entertaining and unpretentious.

Village of the Damned (1960)
Starring George Sanders, Barbara Shelley, Michael Gwynne, Laurence Naismith.
Excellent story of telepathic children.

Visit to a Small Planet (1960)
Starring Jerry Lewis, Joan Blackman, Earl Holliman, Gale Gordon.
Sprightly satire falls prey to Lewis's shenanigans and weak direction by Norman Taurog. Still, it's not bad.

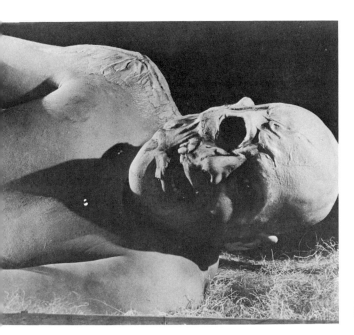

Voyage to a Prehistoric Planet (1964)
Starring Faith Domergue, Basil Rathbone.
Excellent Russian-made trip to Venus. Best of this type.

Voyage to the Bottom of the Sea (1961)
Starring Walter Pidgeon, Michael Ansara, Barbara Eden, Joan Fontaine, Robert Sterling, Peter Lorre, Frankie Avalon.
All-star cast in Irwin Allen's pre–*Poseidon Adventure* end-of-the-world film. Pidgeon and crew of submarine *Seaview* race to North Pole to stop Earth from frying. Fun and well made.

Voyage to the End of the Universe (1964)
Starring Sdenek Stepanek, Radovan Lukavský, Dana Medricka.
Excellent account of the voyage of a huge starship. High-quality production.

War of the Colossal Beast (1958)
Starring Glenn Langan.
Very good Bert I. Gordon sequel to *Amazing Colossal Man*. Acting is especially fine.

War of the Worlds (1953)
Starring Gene Barry, Les Tremayne, Ann Robinson.
Were it not for the astounding special effects, the film would be worthless.

Way, Way Out (1966)
Starring Jerry Lewis, Connie Stevens, Dick Shawn, Robert Morley.
Moderately diverting tale of first man and woman to live on the moon. Some solid laughs . . . but not many.

Westworld (1973)
Starring Yul Brynner, Dick Benjamin.
Michael Crichton wrote and directed this tale of an adult Disneyland of the future. Not what it could have been; Crichton's eye for the technical reduces the film to a sterile narrative.

When Worlds Collide (1951)
Starring Richard Derr, Barbara Rush, John Hoyt.
Excellent film of the Phillip Wylie classic; Pal's special effects won a deserved Oscar.

World, the Flesh and the Devil (1959)
Starring Harry Belafonte, Mel Ferrer, Inger Stevens.
Post–World War III disaster. *Five* remains the definitive work of this sort.

World without End (1956)
Starring Hugh Marlowe, Nancy Gates, Rod Taylor.
Astronauts slip into the future and a world on which mutants battle human beings. It's a good film!

Zombies of the Stratosphere (1952)
Starring Judd Holdren, Aline Towne, Wilson Wood.
Inept serial pastiche.

Glenn Langan is bound to a straw bed in a Los Angeles Airport hangar in War of the Colossal Beast.

233

Films and their Studios

Abbott and Costello Go to Mars   *Universal*
Absent-Minded Professor   *Disney*
Aelita   *Amkino/Vufku/Mezrabpom*
Alligator People   *Fox*
Alphaville   *Pathé-Contemporary/
    Chaumiane-Filmstudio*
Amazing Colossal Man   *American International*
Amazing Transparent Man   *American International*
Andromeda Strain   *Universal*
Angry Red Planet   *American International*
Around the World Under the Sea   *MGM*
Atom Man vs. Superman   *Columbia*
Atomic Submarine   *Allied Artists*
Attack of the Crab Monsters   *Allied Artists*
Attack of the Fifty Foot Woman   *Allied Artists*

Battle Beneath the Earth   *MGM*
Battle for the Planet of the Apes   *Fox*
Battle in Outer Space   *Columbia/Toho*
Beast from Twenty Thousand Fathoms   *Warner Bros.*
Beast With a Million Eyes   *American Releasing Corp.*
Before I Hang   *Columbia*
Beginning of the End   *Republic*
Beneath the Planet of the Apes   *Fox*
Beyond the Time Barrier   *American International*
Black Scorpion   *Warner Bros.*
The Blob   *Paramount*
Blood Beast from Outer Space
    World Entertainment/New Art
Brain From Planet Arous   *Howco International*
Breaking the Sound Barrier   *British Lion*
Bride of Frankenstein   *Universal*
Buck Rogers   *Universal*

Catwoman of the Moon   *Astor*
A Clockwork Orange   *Warner Bros.*
Colossus of New York   *Paramount*
Conquest of Space   *Paramount*
Conquest of the Planet of the Apes   *Fox*
Crack in the World   *Paramount*
Crawling Eye   *DCA*
Creature From the Black Lagoon   *Universal*
Creature Walks Among Us   *Universal*
Creeping Unknown   *United Artists/Hammer*
Curse of Frankenstein   *Warner Bros./Hammer*

Daleks: Invasion Earth 2150 A.D.   *Amicus*
Day Mars Invaded Earth   *Fox/API*
Day of the Triffids   *Allied Artists*

Day the Earth Caught Fire   *Universal*
Day the Earth Stood Still   *Fox*
Deadly Mantis   *Universal*
Destination: Inner Space   *Magna/United*
Destination Moon   *United Artists*
Devil Commands   *Columbia*
Dr. Strangelove   *Columbia*
Dr. Who and the Daleks   *Amicus*
Dr. X   *First National*
Donovan's Brain   *United Artists*

Earth vs. the Flying Saucers   *Columbia*
Enemy From Space   *United Artists/Hammer*
Escape From the Planet of the Apes   *Fox*
Evil of Frankenstein   *Universal/Hammer*

Fahrenheit 451   *Universal*
Fail Safe   *Columbia*
Fantastic Voyage   *Fox*
Fire Maidens of Outer Space   *Eros/Criterion/Topaz*
First Spaceship on Venus   *Crown/Defa-Film/Polski*
Five   *Columbia*
Five Million Years to Earth   *Fox/Hammer*
Flame Barrier   *United Artists*
Flash Gordon   *Universal*
Flash Gordon Conquers the Universe   *Universal*
Flash Gordon's Trip to Mars   *Universal*
The Fly   *Fox*
Flying Disc Man From Mars   *Republic*
Forbidden Planet   *MGM*
The Forbin Project   *Universal*
The 4-D Man   *Universal*
Four-Sided Triangle   *United Artists/Hammer*
Frankenstein   *Universal*
Frankenstein 1970   *Allied Artists*
From the Earth to the Moon   *Warner Bros./RKO*

Gamma People   *Columbia*
Ghidrah   *Toho*
Giant Behemoth   *Allied Artists*
Giant Claw   *Columbia*
Giant Gila Monster   *Hollywood Pictures*
Gigantis   *Warner Bros./Toho*
Girl in the Moon   *UFA*
Godzilla   *Embassy/Jewel/Toho*
Gog   *United Artists*
Gorgo   *MGM*
Green Slime   *MGM*

The completed Space Ark, ready for takeoff. From When Worlds Collide.

Have Rocket Will Travel   *Columbia*

I Married a Monster From Outer Space   *Paramount*
Incredible Shrinking Man   *Universal*
Invaders From Mars   *Fox*
Invasion of the Body Snatchers   *Allied Artists*
Invasion of the Saucer Men   *American International*
Invasion of the Star Creatures   *American International*
Invisible Boy   *MGM*
Invisible Man   *Universal*
Island of Lost Souls   *Paramount*
It Came From Beneath the Sea   *Columbia*
It Conquered the World   *American International*
It! The Terror From Beyond Space   *United Artists*

Journey to the Center of the Earth   *Fox*
Journey to the Far Side of the Sun   *Universal*
Journey to the Seventh Planet   *American International*
Just Imagine   *Fox*

Killers From Space   *RKO*
King Dinosaur   *Lippert/Zingor*
King Kong vs. Godzilla   *Universal/Toho*

King of the Rocket Men   *Republic*
Konga   *American International*
Kronos   *Fox*

Man From Planet X   *United Artists*
Man Made Monster   *Universal*
Man They Could Not Hang   *Columbia*
Man With Nine Lives   *Columbia*
Man With the X-Ray Eyes   *American International*
The Manster   *Luper/Shaw-Breakston*
Marooned   *Columbia*
Metropolis   *Paramount*
Missile to the Moon   *Astor*
Monolith Monsters   *Universal*
Monster That Challenged the World   *United Artists*
Moon Zero Two   *Warner Bros—Hammer*
Mothra   *Columbia/Toho*
Mouse on the Moon   *Lopert*
Mysterious Dr. Satan   *Republic*
Mysterious Island   *Columbia*

1984   *Columbia*
Nutty Professor   *Paramount*

Omega Man   *Warner Bros.*
On the Beach   *United Artists*

Panic in the Year Zero
American International/Alta Vista
Phantom Creeps   Universal
Phantom Empire   Mascot
Phantom Planet   American International
Plan Nine From Outer Space   DCA
Planet of the Apes   Fox
The Power   MGM
Purple Monster Strikes   Republic

Queen of Outer Space   Allied Artists

Radar Men From the Moon   Republic
Red Planet Mars   United Artists
Reptilicus   American International/Cinemagic
Return of the Fly   Fox
Revenge of the Creature   Universal
Robinson Crusoe on Mars   Paramount
Robot Monster   Astor
Rocketship XM   Lippert
Rodan   Toho

Satan Bug   United Artists
Silent Running   Universal
Slaughterhouse Five   Universal
Son of Frankenstein   Universal
Soylent Green   MGM
Space Children   Paramount
Superman   Columbia
Superman and the Mole Men   Lippert

Tarantula   Universal
Target Earth   Allied Artists
Teenage Caveman   American International
Teenagers From Outer Space   Warner Bros.
Terrornauts   Embassy/Amicus

Artist Robert Rigg's interpretation of the robot monster from The Mysterians.

Them!   Warner Bros.
These Are the Damned   Columbia/Hammer
The Thing   RKO
Things to Come   United Artists
This Island Earth   Universal
Three Stooges in Orbit   Columbia
THX 1138   Warner Bros.
The Time Machine   MGM
Time Travelers   American International
Tobor the Great   Republic
Transatlantic Tunnel   Gaum
A Trip to the Moon   Melies/Star
Twenty Million Miles to Earth   Columbia
27th Day   Columbia
Twenty Thousand Leagues Under the Sea   Disney
2001: A Space Odyssey   MGM
The Twonky   United Artists

Undersea Kingdom   Republic

Village of the Damned   MGM
Visit to a Small Planet   Paramount
Voyage to a Prehistoric Planet   New Realm
Voyage to the Bottom of the Sea   Fox
Voyage to the End of the Universe
American International/Barrandov

War of the Colossal Beast   American International
War of the Worlds   Paramount
Way, Way Out   Fox
Westworld   MGM
When Worlds Collide   Paramount
World, Flesh, and the Devil   MGM
World Without End   Allied Artists

Zombies of the Stratosphere   Republic

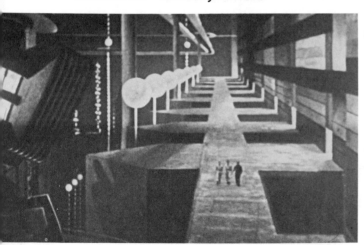

Rare photograph showing the extraordinary Krell machinery miles beneath the surface of the Forbidden Planet.

Notes

1. *Dream of a Rarebit Fiend* was the first film to use a technique that, when it reappeared in *2001: A Space Odyssey,* was considered revolutionary. The protagonist of the earlier, silent film awakes from restless sleep and is chased about his bedroom by food (men in costumes). The man runs from his bed to the wall to the ceiling to the wall and back again, pursued by the bizarre personification, in one continuous take. In reality, of course, the man and the meal were running in place, the room and the camera mounted therein doing all the turning.
    This technique was used again by Fred Astaire in a rather startling dance number and finally by Kubrick when a stewardess, under weightless conditions, walks from the floor through a doorway in the ceiling.

2. Split screen is one of the more simple special-effects techniques. A portion of the lens is masked by a cutaway lens cover. The film is exposed and rewound. The film is reexposed, this time the previously masked portion being exposed and the exposed portion now masked. Through this technique, Patty Duke was able to play both herself and her cousin in *The Patty Duke Show.*

3. A matte—French for "mask"—is a widely used form of superimposition. If we wish to place a flying saucer over the skies of Washington, D.C., the first step is to shoot the background—buildings, sky, etc. Next, the flying saucer is mounted with wires in front of a process screen, a special screen that doesn't photograph. We shoot as much of the saucer as we need, and the footage is then developed into two prints. One is normal; the other is exposed until it becomes a solid black image of the saucer on the transparent process-screen background. This black print is our matte. The three strips—background, matte, and flying saucer—are then run through an optical printer and photographed on one strip of film, the matte sandwiched between the saucer and the background. Since the saucer is an image on film, were it placed directly on the background without the matte, it would be transparent. When a matte operation isn't performed with precision, the matte tends to wind up slightly larger than the object to be superimposed. This is why, on occasion, a black matte line is visible around an object.

4. Many serials were butchered and rereleased as feature-length films. Some of the more popular reissues were: *Flash Gordon* became *Rocketship* and *Spaceship to the Unknown; Flash Gordon's Trip to Mars* became *Mars Attacks the World; Flash Gordon Conquers the Universe* became *The Purple Death; Buck Rogers* became *Planet Outlaws;* and *Zombies of the Stratosphere* became *Satan's Satellites.*

5. Second-unit directors are responsible for the rough-and-tumble work in a motion picture. They stage, execute, and direct battle scenes, large movements of people and animals, and action sequences.

6. In certain instances, the mood and personality of a film will belong to a decade other than that in which it was made. Rather than be ruled strictly by chronology, wherever

Raymond Massey as Oswald Cabal in Things to Come.

necessary, we have grouped certain films by trend and type rather than by specific dates.

7. It is difficult to say, of course, whether the parting of the Red Sea is more effective than the Monster from the Id. The farce of the Oscars is, of course, that favoritism and not excellence is too often the Academy's voting criterion. Surely, in the 1972 awards Peter O'Toole in *The Ruling Class* stood hardly a chance of winning the Best Actor award over the popular Marlon Brando *Godfather* portrayal. Yet, there is no doubt but that O'Toole's performance was one of the greatest ever, and Brando's was merely adequate.

Indeed, despite innovations in the field that equal the contributions of Walt Disney, not one of Ray Harryhausen's solo efforts has ever won the special-effects Oscar. Yet I doubt whether five films have ever been made to compare with the expertise and brilliance of the special effects in *Jason and the Argonauts*.

8. Science fiction seems to have become inseparably linked with having a message or being profound. That science fiction lends itself to that sort of thing, because it deals with dimensional distortions, reviving the dead, and such, cannot be helped. But this does not negate the genre's value as entertainment. Films such as *This Island Earth* and *Invasion of the Body Snatchers* are precisely entertainment movies. Less trying entertainment are *Fire Maidens of Outer Space* and *Beast from Twenty Thousand Fathoms*.

9. Many CinemaScope and wide-screen motion pictures are rendered impotent by the television screen. *Forbidden Planet* and *This Island Earth* are prime examples. In a wide-screen film, actors may address one another from opposite ends of the screen. In a theater, the large screen can accommodate the panoramic image. A small television screen cannot. In order to present a CinemaScope film on TV, what is known as a TV print must be made. This is a duplicate in which portions of the action have been photographed; it is essentially a form of cropping. A segment of the original image is reshot with the proportions of a TV screen in mind. Thus, if two characters are addressing one another from opposite ends of the screen, the TV print will first feature one of the players speaking and then cut to the other character answering. This is annoying, to say the least.

Additionally, TV is wont to butcher a film. In a recent broadcast of *Ben-Hur*, the first ten minutes were dropped—the nativity sequence. Not as important, CBS must have decided, as an ad for Dog Yummies. Also, there is a great dilution of image on a TV screen, for the picture is broken into small dots that are reconstructed by your picture tube. These dots are painfully evident in TV screenings. Finally, commercial breaks destroy the natural, planned flow of films. So if you can, see movies before they are sold to television..

10. It is strange that the battle between the Ymir and the elephant in *Twenty Million Miles to Earth* far surpasses a similar sequence in Harryhausen's 1969 film, *Valley of Gwangi*, wherein an elephant is engaged in combat by an allosaurus. The elephant in *Valley of Gwangi* is far from realistic—one of the flaws that haunts that film. Rumor has it that a wrong film stock was ordered by Producer Schneer. This would account for Gwangi's changing from green to blue to brown to green at different points in the film.

11. Dynamation is Ray Harryhausen's patented technique of combining live actors with his animated models for the most realistic effects. It was first used in *Twenty Million Miles to Earth* and allowed for the first effective color monster film of this sort, *Seventh Voyage of Sinbad*, in 1958. Edward Nassour's *Beast of Hollow Mountain* (1956), based on Willis O'Brien's idea for the original *Valley of Gwangi* (never filmed, and the basis for the Harryhausen film), used a crude color stop motion–live action combination, but the effect was only occasionally satisfying.

12. In a mid-1973 appearance on *The Dick Cavett Show*, Brando indicated that anyone who thinks film is an art form is crazy. One cannot help but feel—after Brando's brilliant performances in such films as *On the Waterfront* and *One Eyed Jacks*—that he was merely being sensational.

13. Unlike absolute music, absolute film does not necessarily mean surrealistic film. The motion picture in absolute film can still tell a story; it does, however, wholly involve the viewer in its aesthetic—as opposed to pedestrian—use of film as art. Pedestrian is not meant, here, to be derogatory; it is merely the difference between, for instance, *Dr. Strangelove* and the more routine—as film art—*Seven Days in May*.

14. There are those who claim that Kubrick glorifies violence in *A Clockwork Orange*. Although I certainly do not think this was Kubrick's intent, the fact remains that

society—and not violence—is on trial. Although Kubrick is indirectly condemning the violence that is Alex's meat, his artistic use of violence tends to cloud his intent. This is, to an extent, irresponsibility on his part. To hold society up to examination is one thing; to chance having people laugh at rape because of the director's tongue-in-cheek treatment of the elements surrounding it is at best questionable.

15. Anthony Zerbe has long played second fiddle—as have many character actors—to the stars. Zerbe appeared with Heston prior to *Omega Man* in *Will Penny*.

16. Ray Harryhausen recently commented that *Valley of Gwangi*—a G-rated film—was paired on a double bill with an R-rated film. Any fool would realize that the potential audience for *Valley of Gwangi* lies in the "kiddie matinee" trade. Since children are not allowed to see an R-rated film without parental accompaniment, the Harryhausen film had relatively few viewers. Not surprisingly, *Valley of Gwangi* did its best business in the Midwest, where the cowboys-versus-monsters theme was obviously popular. Harryhausen further notes that the man responsible for this double billing was subsequently made a vice-president of Columbia Pictures.

The monster squid in Twenty Thousand Leagues Under the Sea.